**A 1792 law had officially denied blacks the right to become soldiers.**

However, President Lincoln let it be known that once the Emancipation Proclamation took effect, African Americans would be encouraged to join Union forces. Many black men could barely wait to sign up.

"I will draw my sword against my oppressor and the oppressors of my race," a freed slave living in Pennsylvania said, echoing the feelings of many black men. "I will sacrifice everything in order to save the gift of freedom for my race."

# A Background Note about
*A NATION DIVIDED: The American Civil War*

In July of 2000, more than 145 years after the end of the Civil War, there was another battle in South Carolina, the same state where the war began. For many decades, the Confederate flag (the flag of the South during the Civil War) had flown over the state capitol. Some people thought it was a symbol of history and heritage, but many others felt it was a symbol of racism. After much arguing, the flag was finally removed, only to be placed instead directly in front of the capitol. To many African Americans, this was an obvious insult. A boycott of the state by the NAACP (National Association for the Advancement of Colored People) continues to this day.

Although the Civil War took place several generations ago, it is not a dull and dusty history lesson about an event that has no effect on the United States today. The only war ever fought between Americans, the Civil War brought freedom to millions of slaves, changed the South forever, and kept the United States from becoming two separate countries. It was a war of tremendously strong emotions on both sides, and to this day, as witnessed in South Carolina, some of these emotions are still very intense.

In this book, you will follow the story of the Civil War from the first shots fired at Fort Sumter, South Carolina, at the war's beginning, to the single shot fired at Abraham Lincoln after the war's end. You will visit historic battlefields, where you will meet heroes on each side of the conflict, and share their heartbreak and victory. And in the end, you will understand why an old flag from the United States' bloodiest war still compels people to choose a side and argue 145 years later.

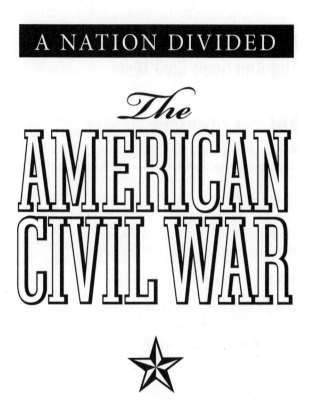

# A NATION DIVIDED

## The AMERICAN CIVIL WAR

# MARK THOMAS

 THE TOWNSEND LIBRARY

# A NATION DIVIDED:
## The American Civil War

**TP** THE TOWNSEND LIBRARY

For more titles in the Townsend Library,
visit our website: **www.townsendpress.com**

Copyright © 2011 by Townsend Press.
Printed in the United States of America

0 9 8 7 6 5 4 3 2 1

Illustrations © 2011 by Hal Taylor

**Townsend Press, Inc.**
**439 Kelley Drive**
**West Berlin, NJ 08091**
**permissions@townsendpress.com**

ISBN-13: 978-1-59194-248-1
ISBN-10: 1-59194-248-9

Library of Congress Control Number:
2011928355

# CONTENTS

# CHAPTER 1

*I*n 1860, two brothers found themselves in an argument that seemed to have no end and no common ground. Growing up in a small town in North Carolina, Henry and his younger brother, Will, had been inseparable best friends, but now there was a bitterness between them, and it grew worse as they argued throughout the long, hot summer.

"How can you dare go back to New York in the fall?" Will demanded. "With the way things are, you should be ashamed."

"*Ashamed*?" Henry cried angrily. "I'm a cadet at West Point, learning to serve my country. I'd hardly call that shameful."

Will just shook his head. "What you call your country is not what I'd call *my* country. You know as well as I do that the government and Northerners want to force their rules and

1

laws on us down here and destroy the way we live. If you want to serve anything, you should serve your home. Doesn't where you come from mean anything to you?"

"You just don't understand it, do you?" Henry fired back, his voice getting louder. "We all live in one country. The states are not separate countries! That's the way it is, and that's the way it's going to stay."

"Maybe not. Everyone in town says that if Abe Lincoln gets elected President, the South will form its own country and its own government," Will countered. "We'll leave the United States altogether."

"Not without one hell of a fight you won't," Henry shouted. "And I don't need to tell you which side I'll be on."

Will folded his arms and glared at his brother. "Well then, I reckon I'll see you on the battlefield— on the opposite side."

Henry just turned and walked away. As angry as he was, he was mostly sad. He and Will had had their share of fights over the years, but nothing that couldn't be worked out in some way. Making matters worse, their father sided with Will. Just that morning, he had looked at Henry and sternly ordered him to remain in North Carolina and stand by his family, his home, and the South.

"No sir," Henry had said quietly. "I have to do

what I feel is right. I won't fight against my own country if that's what it comes to."

"Then you're not the son I thought you were," his father said, his voice trembling. With that, he had left the room, slamming the door behind him.

Now, Will called out to Henry, demanding a response to another argument. But Henry just kept walking. He didn't feel like fighting anymore with the brother he loved. And he didn't want Will to see the tears in his eyes.

How had it gotten to this point of brothers fighting brothers? Barely eighty years earlier, Americans had struggled together in the Revolutionary War, fighting for their freedom from British rule. United in vision and direction, Americans had named themselves "the United States." Now, just a few generations later, Americans were bitterly divided within the country, within states, and even within families. Many people in the South did not think of themselves as being part of a united country.

The troubles and disagreements that led to the Civil War were many. It is difficult to say that one specific thing caused the war. Northern states were richer, more populated, and more advanced in industry. This made Southerners both a little envious and a little worried. Furthermore, many people in the South felt that each individual state should be allowed to make its own laws and not be bound to what the federal government decided. Because Washington, D.C., the nation's capital, was in the North, Southerners began to suspect that Northerners, or "Yankees," were becoming too powerful. Many worried that it was only a matter of time until the North would take over the South.

But the longest-fought issue and the one that most strongly divided people was the issue of slavery.

"I think we must get rid of slavery, or we must get rid of freedom," declared the famous writer Ralph Waldo Emerson.

Many Americans—even some in the South— agreed with Emerson. But those who disagreed, disagreed bitterly.

"It is our constitutional right to own slaves!" Southern slaveholders argued. And they were right. When the Constitution had been written in 1787, most Southern states had refused to agree to it unless slavery was protected. At the time, it didn't seem like such a big deal. After all, even Thomas Jefferson owned hundreds of slaves. And Americans had been bringing slaves over from Africa since 1620—why change now? Finally, the founding fathers decided to let the issue of slavery slide. They pointed out that there weren't that many slaves in the South anyway. Aside from seasonal work on a handful of rice, indigo, and tobacco farms, there really wasn't a great need for slaves.

Then, barely seven years after the Constitution was approved and signed, that all changed.

A young inventor from Massachusetts named Eli Whitney visited the South and noticed that while cotton seemed easy to grow, few farmers planted it. There was always a tremendously bigger demand for cotton than the South could supply. The problem, Whitney discovered, was in the cotton itself. Dozens of little seeds filled each cotton ball, and removing them was a slow and difficult process.

Eli Whitney instantly saw dollar signs. If he could invent a machine that removed the seeds, both he and Southern farmers would become incredibly rich. In two weeks, Whitney had drawn up a design. Within the year, the cotton engine, or cotton "gin," had become a reality.

To say that the cotton gin made Southern farmers rich is an understatement. Suddenly, cotton production skyrocketed. Instead of taking days to clean the cotton, it took only hours. Farmers greatly increased their acreage and became known as "planters." And their simple farmhouses were transformed into magnificent plantations with tall white columns and unending luxuries.

However, the prosperity of the planters created suffering for the slaves. Cotton was a plant that required a lot of attention as it grew and a lot of work to harvest. As a result, the slave trade from Africa tripled and then quadrupled. Throughout the South, the slave population grew from 700,000 in 1790 to 4,000,000 in 1860. One out of every three people living in the South was a slave. And as the demand for cotton continued to increase, slaves were forced to work harder and harder.

At the same time, the slave population in the North had steadily grown smaller. With the invention of new machinery in the factories, less manual labor was needed, and so slaves were often allowed to buy their freedom. Some Northern slave owners simply freed their slaves and then hired them for low-paying positions. In any event, the absence of slavery in the North drew attention to how cruel and out-of-control the institution of slavery had become in the South.

Sharpening this focus were the horrifying stories told by runaway slaves who escaped from the plantations to states north of the Mason-Dixon Line (the line that separated slave states from free states). Not all slave owners were unkind, but some starved, beat, and even raped their slaves.

"You don't do your task, Master will wave that whip, put you over a barrel, and beat you so blood run down," a slave from South Carolina grimly explained.

"Master told me I was his property," a fifteen-year-old slave girl related. "Said I must be subject to his will in all things. *All* things. He was a vile, disgusting monster."

The life of a slave involved backbreaking work from sunup to sundown. It was an existence of fear and ongoing heartache. Because slaves were bought and sold like livestock, families were often separated. It was not unusual for a child to be snatched from the arms of his or her mother if the buyer didn't want a "full set" of slaves. Most slaves were housed in cabins that were little more than flimsy stables with dirt floors. Meals consisted of coarse corn meal and pork fat.

"Was no fruit or anything else, even though there be fields of fruit trees and vegetables surrounding Master's house," an elderly escaped slave from Virginia reported. "We dare not steal the fruit. We seen what happens. Master done hang a young boy by the neck from the very tree where he took an apple."

In their misery, many slaves expressed the desire to be dead rather than to continue being a slave. Sadly, this wish often came true soon enough. In 1850, the life expectancy of a black man in some parts of the South was only twenty-nine years.

As Southern slaveholders tried to defend their right to buy and sell human beings, the voices of the abolitionists (those who wanted to abolish, or do away with, slavery) grew louder. Those who supported slavery claimed that they were actually doing the slaves a favor by taking them away from the "wicked and savage" land of Africa.

"They are fed, given homes, and taught the Bible," was the standard response. "They're better off here than where they are from. They should be thankful to their masters!"

This line of thinking made Abraham Lincoln exceptionally angry. "Whenever I hear anyone arguing for slavery, I feel a strong impulse to see it tried on him personally," Lincoln once commented.

In the North, many agreed with Lincoln. Abolitionists believed that black people deserved to be treated with the same fairness that any American citizen expected. But then, in 1857, the Supreme Court ruled that neither slaves nor descendants of slaves could be United States citizens. Furthermore, it was ruled that the federal government could not prohibit slavery in U.S. territories, such as Kansas and Nebraska. Instead, settlers in those territories could decide for themselves whether or not to allow slavery.

The Chief Justice of the Supreme Court, a former slave owner from Maryland, argued that these new laws simply followed the Constitution.

"It must be followed now as it was written then," he proclaimed. "Until the point at which it is amended, the Constitution and its laws cannot be changed."

This was true, but it made abolitionists furious.

"Slavery, throughout its entire existence in the United States is none other than the most barbarous, unprovoked, and unjustifiable war of one portion of its citizens upon another portion. It is in utter disregard and violation of those eternal and self-evident truths set forth in our Declaration of Independence."

These were the angry words of John Brown, a wild-eyed and radical abolitionist from Connecticut. Brown was tired of talk and laws and red tape. He wanted change, and he was willing to kill for it. Along with several of his older sons (he had a lot of children), Brown rushed to Kansas, where there had already been so much fighting between pro-slavery and anti-slavery groups that Kansas had been nicknamed "Bloody Kansas." Without warning, Brown and his sons burst into the homes of five unarmed pro-slavery men and slaughtered them with knives and swords.

Then, in 1859, Brown and a group of his followers, called "raiders," took over a United States weapons arsenal in the town of Harper's Ferry in Virginia, a slave state. Brown's plan was to give the guns and ammunition to slaves, who would, in turn, murder their masters. Brown believed that once enough slaves were armed, slave owners throughout the South would be so terrorized that they would be happy to free their slaves.

It didn't turn out quite that way.

Brown and his men managed to raid the arsenal, but the slaves were reluctant to fight against their masters. Not one slave would take a gun. As Brown and his raiders tried to figure out what to do next, angry townspeople surrounded the arsenal and began throwing bricks at Brown and his men. Brown attempted to run free, but was trapped by the crowd. Convicted of treason and murder, Brown was ultimately led to the gallows to be hanged.

Just before his execution he handed a guard a piece of paper on which he had written this message: "The crimes of this guilty land will never be purged away but with blood!"

It was his prediction of war, and now he was not alone in the belief that only war could ease the growing tension in the United States. Most Northerners and abolitionists had not approved of Brown's violent approach. Abolitionists were generally peaceful and thoughtful individuals who just wanted to see all people treated fairly. Even so, they understood John Brown's anger, and some even pointed to him as a hero who had made the ultimate sacrifice.

On the other hand, Southerners pointed to Brown and said, "Look! This is what everyone up North wants to do! They plan to murder us, go against the Constitution, and force us to give up our slaves." Bloody skirmishes flared more often in border states (the five slave states that bordered free states but remained loyal to the United States: Delaware, Kentucky, Maryland, Missouri, and West

Virginia). Families took sides against one another. And a Southern congressman, Preston Brooks, became so furious with an anti-slavery Northern senator, Charles Sumner, that he beat him senseless with his cane right in the middle of the Senate floor.

"I wore my cane out completely," Brooks announced proudly. "But I saved the gold handle." Merchants in South Carolina applauded their senator's actions and bought him a new cane. Inscribed in the wood of the cane were these words: "Hit him again."

By mid-1860, the tension between the North and the South was nearing a breaking point. Talk of leaving the Union (the combined states of the United States) began rumbling in the South. Many people could sense the edge of war creeping nearer and nearer.

"We knew it was just a matter of time," said a farmer from Alabama. "Me and my boys were ready. Just didn't know what would set it off."

What finally "set it off" was the election of the United States' sixteenth President, Abraham Lincoln. Many Southerners believed that Lincoln was dead set on immediately freeing all slaves and turning the South into an extension of the North. Some envisioned swarms of Yankees rushing down to destroy plantations and replace them with factories, all with Lincoln's blessing.

In reality, nothing could have been further from the truth. Lincoln believed slavery was wrong, and he was against allowing it to spread to new states. Still, he understood Southerners' worries. He realized that suddenly abolishing slavery would destroy the South's economy. Lincoln cared deeply about the United States as a whole; he had no greater love for the North than he did for the South. He wasn't about to do anything drastic.

"Wrong as we think slavery is," he had said while campaigning, "we can yet afford to let it alone where it is."

Southerners, however, were not convinced. If the President thought slavery was wrong, he would find a way, eventually, to get rid of it altogether. Then, many agreed, the South would fall to ruin. In the presidential election, Lincoln did not receive a majority of votes in any Southern state. Although he narrowly won the election, it was the first time an American President had been elected without any support from the South. Lincoln knew what that meant.

"Well, boys, your troubles are over now," Lincoln wryly said to weary reporters who had been covering the election nonstop, "but mine have just begun."

Within weeks and even before Lincoln was inaugurated, South Carolina responded by seceding, or breaking away, from the Union. South Carolina was followed by six other states: Mississippi, Florida, Alabama, Georgia, Louisiana, and Texas. These states banded together and formed a new country that they named the Confederate States of America (also called "the Confederacy"). Before long, they would be joined by Virginia, Arkansas, Tennessee, and North Carolina.

Two years earlier, Lincoln had been speaking about slavery when he had said:

"'A house divided against itself cannot stand.' I believe this government cannot endure, permanently, half slave and half free. I do not expect the Union to be dissolved—I do not expect the house to fall—but I do expect it will cease to be divided. It will become all one thing or all the other."

But now people in the South had taken matters into their own hands and divided the "house" in a very real way. They had, in fact, dissolved the Union by creating their own country.

In Washington, D.C., the newly elected President was reported to have put his head in his hands when he received the news. Days later, he stood on the Capitol steps in front of thousands and delivered his inaugural address.

"Plainly, the central idea of secession is the essence of anarchy," he said sternly of the South's decision to secede. "No State, upon its own mere motion, can lawfully get out of the Union. . . . They can only do so against the law, and by revolution."

At the same time, Lincoln attempted to reach out to the South. "We must not be enemies," he pleaded.

But the South was concerned neither about breaking the laws of a country it had rejected nor about being friends with that "other" country. And even as Lincoln spoke in Washington, Confederate troops were forming in Charleston, South Carolina. The revolution was about to begin.

## CHAPTER 2

*A*t 4:30 in the morning on April 12, 1861, a young woman named Mary Chesnut was awakened by what sounded like the most tremendous thunder she had ever heard. It shook the windows of her home near the harbor of Charleston, South Carolina. She jumped out of bed and immediately fell to her knees. She knew that what she was hearing was not thunder.

"I prayed as I never prayed before," Mary would later write. Like many Southerners, Mary did not necessarily support slavery, but she did support the South's desire for independence from the North. Mary was frightened by the idea of fighting "so great a power as the U.S.A.," but now the moment had arrived.

After praying, Mary rushed up the stairs to the roof of her home, where there was a narrow walkway. She stood staring out toward the sea. A mighty blaze of yellow and red filled the dark sky near the small island of Fort Sumter. Ever since the Revolutionary War, Fort Sumter had guarded the vulnerable entrance to Charleston Harbor, but now it was being bombarded with shells and cannonballs.

However, it was the South that was attacking Fort Sumter, not the North.

Sumter, like a number of forts in the South, was United States property. Therefore, it was under the control and command of the Union, now the enemy of the Confederacy.

Earlier in the year, before Lincoln had taken office as President, Governor Francis Pickens of South Carolina had written to then President Buchanan demanding that all federal property in South Carolina, including Fort Sumter, be given up. Governor Pickens thought that a Union fort in his state—in one of the Confederacy's most important harbors—would be a serious threat.

President Buchanan denied Governor Pickens's demand, but that didn't stop Pickens from repeating it—several times. Buchanan stalled. He recognized the seriousness of the situation, and he didn't want a war to start in the last weeks of his presidency.

About a month after Lincoln was inaugurated on March 4, the issue came to a head: Supplies at Fort Sumter were running low. This posed a dilemma for Lincoln: If he didn't supply the fort (and therefore surrendered it), Northerners would see him as weak; on the other hand, if he sent in troops with the supplies, he would be criticized for being an aggressor. Lincoln found the perfect solution: He indicated that a ship with supplies for Fort Sumter was on its way. Lincoln was careful to point out, however, that there were no troops or munitions aboard the ship. It should not be considered a threat.

It didn't matter. A Union fort in the South was threat enough. Newly appointed president of the Confederacy, Jefferson Davis, gave the go-ahead to begin attacking the fort if it did not surrender by 4:30 a.m. on April 12. Major Robert Anderson, the Union commander of Fort Sumter, refused to give up his fort, and he told his troops to prepare for an attack.

"Strike a blow!" The shouts of the Confederates manning the guns and cannons on nearby islands filled the air as the deadline for surrender came and went. For nearly two days, screaming shells and thudding cannonballs rained down upon Fort Sumter.

"It seemed impossible to escape the suffocation," a captain at Fort Sumter wrote. "The roaring and crackling of the flames, the dense masses of swirling smoke, and the bursting of the enemy's shells . . . made the fort a pandemonium."

In Charleston, residents lined rooftops and watched the show of lights and smoke of the bombardment. As word spread that the South was winning this first battle, some of the rooftop watching turned into rooftop partying. Champagne was poured, and fancy hors d'oeuvres were served. Finally, when Fort Sumter began running out of ammunition, Major Anderson realized that there was no way he could win. On the afternoon of April 13, the United States flag came down, and a white flag was raised over Sumter.

Surrender. The Confederates had won.

Mary Chesnut was so excited and exhausted from a day and a half on her rooftop that she sat right down on her chimney, nearly lighting her dress on fire. Later that evening, she wrote in her diary: "Do you know, after all that noise and our tears and prayers, nobody has been hurt . . . after the dread of all the slaughter we thought those dreadful cannons were making such a noise in doing."

The thick stone walls of Fort Sumter had protected the men within them, and the barricades on the islands had done the same for the Confederates. Amazingly, not one soldier had been seriously injured. This would be the only battle of the Civil War with such astonishing luck.

In Washington, a grim Abraham Lincoln sent out the order to "repossess the forts . . . which have been seized from the Union." This could mean only one thing:

"War! War! War!"

The streets of Richmond, Virginia, overflowed with young men shouting and chanting. Several weeks later, the capital of the Confederacy was moved from Montgomery, Alabama, to Richmond—and for good reason. Placing this new center of government only 100 miles from Washington, D.C., served as both a threat and a taunt. It was the Confederacy's way of showing that it was not afraid to put itself right on the Union's doorstep.

Now, in both the South and the North, young men could not run fast enough to sign up to fight. Union recruits were angry that the South had considered the taking over of Fort Sumter "winning" a battle.

"The President will soon fix them," a young man from Indiana said of Lincoln's decision to go to war. "Just as soon as those fellows find out that the North means business, they will get down off their high horse."

Lincoln had called for 75,000 soldiers to volunteer for just three months of service. Although Lincoln had lingering doubts, the general feeling was that the North would win this war quickly. How could it not? It was stronger and richer, and had nearly triple the population of the South. The "Rebels" in the South, so named because of their rebellious nature, saw things very differently.

"Those Union leaders in Washington, D.C., want to destroy the South," one Confederate complained angrily. "I'd rather die than become a slave to the North."

Very few soldiers, however, spoke of slavery as a reason for going to war. Northern soldiers simply wanted to support their President and their country—and keep the Union whole. Southern soldiers wanted to defend their homes from what they felt was an unfair and meddling government and, now, an invading army. In reality, only about fifteen percent of Southerners actually owned slaves. The majority of Southerners in 1861 were farmers with very little land and even less money.

"I do not know anything about it," one Confederate soldier admitted when asked about slavery. "Whether it's a good thing or a bad thing, I just don't know."

What soldiers *did* know, however, was that they could not wait to go into battle.

"So impatient did I become," wrote a volunteer from Arkansas, "that I felt like ten thousand pins were pricking me in every part of my body!"

When the Confederacy's President Davis heard that President Lincoln had asked for 75,000 volunteers, Davis asked for 60,000 men to fight for the South. Neither president had any trouble getting his recruits. Men had to be at least eighteen years old to fight, but so wild was the fever to go to war that boys as young as twelve tried to sign up. They put on men's hats, stuffed rags in their shoes in an attempt to look taller, and marched down to the recruitment centers in the town squares. Back in 1861, verifying someone's actual age was almost impossible—there were no driver's licenses or social security numbers. Some recruiters asked the boys questions or, in some cases, gave their chins a quick rub to see if they had whiskers yet.

Young boys who couldn't fool the recruiters were often offered a different, if less exciting, job. Instead of a gun, they were handed a bugle, or drumsticks and a drum. Thousands of musicians were needed for the war, but they were not for the entertainment of the soldiers. In the 1860s, drumbeats and bugle calls were the main means of communication on the battlefields. A certain series of beats might indicate whether troops should move forward or retreat. Being a drummer boy was an important job, but it did not seem nearly as courageous as fighting.

"I will play this drum," one boy wrote to a friend, "but will sneak into the fight, too. Wait and see!"

"It takes a recruit some time to learn that he is not to think or suggest, but obey," announced a frustrated drill sergeant who was working around the clock with Union troops to get them ready for battle.

Although the Union had significantly more soldiers and better supplies and weaponry than the Confederacy, it lagged behind the Confederacy in preparing recruits for their first battle. Many of the Northern soldiers were from cities or towns, where they worked at trades or in factories. They were not always in particularly good shape, and most of them had rarely, if ever, fired a gun. On the other hand, most of the Southerners came from farms, where they did hours of physical labor every day. Nearly all of them used guns for hunting. When word began trickling down to the Confederates that the Yankees didn't know how to fire a gun, there was much snickering and joking.

"Do not worry, Mother," one Southern recruit wrote in a letter home. "There will be very little danger in battle; the Yankees cannot shoot."

For their part, the Northern recruits made just as much fun of the "boastful, loud-mouthed" Rebels, who they felt were all a bunch of ragged hicks who would turn and run like cowards as soon as they saw the larger, better-equipped Northern armies headed toward them.

But by July of 1861, the time for trading insults and preparing for battle was coming to an end. Abraham Lincoln was worried that if the ninety-day recruits went for ninety days without fighting one battle, both the North and the soldiers would begin losing confidence. Furthermore, a Confederate army of 20,000 men had now moved into northern Virginia, barely twenty miles from Washington, D.C. This was far too close for comfort. The Confederates were gathered near the town of Manassas, along a narrow and overgrown river named Bull Run. Led by General P.G.T. Beauregard, the same general who had led the victory at Fort Sumter, the Rebels were full of confidence, and they were itching for a fight.

"On to Richmond! On to Richmond!" came the shout all over Washington as thousands of Union troops poured into the city to prepare for the march to Bull Run. Most of the soldiers, and even Abraham Lincoln, felt that the Confederates would be easily beaten at Bull Run. From there, it would be a quick march down to Richmond, where the Union army would seize the city and take over the capitol, thereby putting a quick end to this ridiculous Confederate States of America.

Nearly 40,000 Union troops camped out in Washington in the days leading up to the march. It was so crowded that some soldiers slept in government areas, including the Capitol rotunda and the chamber of the House of Representatives. Army tents filled the White House grounds and stretched across the city as far as the eye could see. The last-minute military drills thrilled the residents of Washington, who came out and cheered enthusiastically for every little thing the soldiers did.

One soldier sheepishly wrote home in a letter that he had received a thunderous round of applause simply for cleaning his gun.

Finally it was time to go. As the troops filed out of Washington, music played and fireworks boomed. Women cried, and older men proudly saluted the young soldiers. But once they were miles away from the excitement, many of the soldiers quickly began to grow weary. It was a hot, dusty day, and twenty miles in a wool uniform was exhausting to these new, green recruits.

"They stopped every moment to pick blackberries or drink from the creeks," complained Irvin McDowell, the general in command. "They would not keep in the ranks."

Some of the soldiers simply sat down alongside the road to rest whenever they felt like it. Others took off their packs and tucked them behind trees, claiming they were too heavy to take all the way to Bull Run. Once, when soldiers approached a creek, many of them worried about getting their feet wet.

It was this level of inexperience and softness that made the first Battle of Bull Run so horrifying for so many soldiers on both sides. On the morning of July 21, McDowell's troops advanced toward the Confederates and began shooting through the tangled woods that hung over the river. Men were spread out for miles on either side of Bull Run, hiding behind trees and crouching in ravines.

This was nothing like the battles many soldiers had imagined. All the drills had been on open fields with men in plain sight, almost like a game. But now, as the battle heightened, cannons boomed, and the smoke from thousands of bullets and cannonballs turned the morning sky gray. Horses shrieked in terror, and grown men cried with fear as they moved forward toward the enemy.

Many soldiers panicked.

"I saw a cannonball hit my friend and completely tear his head right off. He wasn't more than ten feet from me," one soldier recalled. "I couldn't even remember how to load my gun after that."

Making matters more confusing amid the fighting was the lack of standard uniforms. In the future, the Union soldiers would wear blue, and the Confederates would wear gray. However, in this first battle, soldiers from both sides often wore the same colors, and hundreds of men were mistakenly shot by their own comrades.

At first, the much larger Union army had the upper hand. Line after line of soldiers kept appearing before the exhausted Confederates. Around noon, the Rebels began retreating slowly and then more quickly as the shout of "Back! Back!" was passed along the lines. The Union's General McDowell stood up in his stirrups on his horse and threw his hat up in the air with a whoop.

"Victory!" he shouted. "Victory! The day is ours."

But unseen by General McDowell was another large brigade of Virginia soldiers led by General Thomas Jackson. Jackson was a harsh, tough leader who demanded obedience and unfailing bravery from his troops. Jackson refused to retreat with the other Confederates. He sat on his horse amid the gunfire and directed the Virginia brigade to move forward instead.

This inspired the retreating Rebels, who stared at Jackson in amazement.

"There is Jackson standing like a stone wall!" shouted one of the commanding officers. "Rally behind the Virginians!"

Not only did Jackson's stance result in his being nicknamed "Stonewall" from that point on, it also turned the tide for the Confederates. With a high-pitched scream that would become known as "the Rebel yell," the Confederates turned back around and began fighting with a new fury. Catching the Union soldiers off guard was exactly what Stonewall Jackson had hoped for. As the Rebels charged with their gleaming bayonets out in front of them, the Union soldiers took their turn at retreat.

What followed next was one of the stranger scenes from the Civil War. On the morning of the battle, hundreds of sightseers from Washington had come to sit on a nearby hillside and watch the fighting, much the way spectators might watch a football game. Many had dressed grandly for the occasion and brought along picnic baskets and fine wines. They had assumed that their side would win quickly and cleanly. There would be some cheering and congratulating followed by a pleasant ride through the country back to Washington.

Hardly.

As the Union troops retreated and the Confederates continued to advance, many Union soldiers panicked. They threw down their guns and ran wildly up the hillside—straight toward the picnickers. In turn, the startled spectators abandoned their lunches and fled the stampede that was heading toward them. Soon, a gigantic mob of soldiers, ladies in frilly dresses, and gentlemen in silk suits was dashing down the dusty road toward Washington. A senator who had taken his shoes off to relax on the hillside ran in his socks for nearly ten miles. It became a joke that his fellow senators would never let him forget.

Back in Washington, however, Abraham Lincoln was not laughing. How on earth, he asked angrily, could the Union possibly have lost this battle? One of Lincoln's top generals, William Tecumseh Sherman, did not offer any excuses.

"The battle was lost by us . . . because our army was as green as grass," he said plainly. Further,

Sherman pointed out, the Southern generals were more daring. They were more willing to take unexpected chances and put their soldiers at risk. Regardless of what people had thought, the Confederates were going to fight hard. Perhaps, Sherman suggested, the North and even the President himself had underestimated just how desperately the South wanted to win this war.

Lincoln thought long and hard about this the entire night. It looked as though this would not be a quick war after all. Enlisting only 75,000 men to fight for only ninety days had clearly been a misjudgment. In the morning, the President put forth a new order.

"The Union must enlist 500,000 men," he announced grimly. "This time they must serve for three years."

# CHAPTER 3

*N*early 5,000 soldiers were killed, wounded, missing, or captured at Bull Run. It was a number that stunned the nation and frightened soldiers. Suddenly, the idea of fighting in a war was no longer appealing. War was real, and it was far more terrible than any new recruit had thought it could be.

After Union troops had retreated completely, dazed Confederate soldiers wandered around the river and fields where the battle had been fought, looking for their fallen friends. Bodies were strewn everywhere.

"Some seem to have had a terrible struggle with the monster Death," wrote one soldier in a letter. "Their expressions are fearful to look upon, their features distorted, their eyeballs glaring, and often their hands full of mud and grass that they clutched in their last agony."

Bull Run itself was tinted red with the blood of the dead, but the exhausted soldiers were so thirsty that they drank it anyway. As they sat on the muddy creek banks, Confederate soldiers stared at one another, wordless and white-faced. Victory was theirs, but it was far more bitter than sweet as the smoke of the battle still hung heavily over the fields.

"And so, at that very moment, we began to think that a battle is not so nice as some had imagined," a drillmaster from Virginia later recalled.

Union soldiers marched slowly back to their camps with their heads down. Some helped the wounded along. Others carried in their heads the dying words of friends to deliver to loved ones. And one soldier grasped a letter tightly in his hand. In part, it read:

> I cannot describe to you my feelings on this calm summer night, when two thousand men are sleeping around me, many of them enjoying the last, perhaps, before that of death—and I, suspicious that Death is creeping behind me with his fatal dart, am communing with God, my country, and thee.

> Sarah, my love for you is deathless, it seems to bind me to you with mighty

cables that nothing but Omnipotence could break; and yet my love of Country comes over me like a strong wind and bears me irresistibly on, with all these chains, to the battlefield.

I pray that I shall return to my loved ones unharmed. If I do not, my dear Sarah, never forget how much I love you, and when my last breath escapes me on the battlefield, it will whisper your name . . . and if there be a soft breeze upon your cheek, it shall be my breath; or the cool air fans your throbbing temple, it shall be my spirit passing by.

The letter had been written by Major Sullivan Ballou only days before the Battle of Bull Run. Like so many Union soldiers, Major Ballou's devotion to his country and to the fight to keep it unified was strong enough to take him from his home and his young wife. And now the man who carried the letter was not Ballou, but rather a soldier intent on delivering a friend's last words of love to his wife.

Ballou's suspicion of death creeping up behind him had proven correct. He had been killed by a musket shot within the first hour of the fighting at Bull Run.

• • •

The Confederate capital of Richmond still remained the jewel that must be captured if the North was going to win the war, but now the cries of "On to Richmond!" had died down. Lincoln and his generals knew it was time to regroup and rebuild. Summer was quickly coming to an end, and neither side was prepared to continue fighting during the winter. And so, the Confederate armies in the east gathered near Richmond to spend the winter, living in either tents or quickly built mud and log cabins. Likewise, the Union armies stayed near Washington.

Still, the war continued elsewhere.

"Whatever nation gets control of the Ohio, Mississippi, and Missouri Rivers, will control the continent," General Sherman had pointed out to Lincoln.

The Confederate states, of course, included more than just the eastern states of Virginia, the Carolinas, Georgia, and Florida. What was known as "the War in the West" continued on through the winter of 1861–1862 as Union armies attempted to capture forts along or near important river routes. Rivers were vital for bringing food and supplies up from southern seaports and into every corner of the South. Additionally, the rivers were the roadways for cotton exports. In particular, European countries bought a tremendous amount of cotton. In return, these countries often sent military supplies and arms that the South needed but had no factories to build.

One top Union commander, Winfield Scott, took a long look at the Union's plan to take over important rivers and thought the Union was going about things backward.

"Send United States Navy ships to all of the Confederate ports instead," he suggested to Lincoln. "If ports are blocked from Virginia all the way around to Texas, no supplies can get in at all. The Confederates will be strangled." When newspapers in the North got wind of Scott's plan, they laughed at it. For one thing, the blockading of ports would take a long time, and most people still felt that this war would be over within the year. The South probably had enough supplies to last a year, so what would be the point of these blockades anyway?

Scott had been nicknamed "Old Fuss and Feathers" because he was known to love ceremony and big productions. Now, his idea was looked at as just another overblown and unnecessary event. Newspapers drew cartoons poking fun at Scott's plan, sketching a huge snake that wrapped 3,500 miles around the South, trying to strangle it. As a joke, Scott's idea was named "the Anaconda Plan."

Lincoln, however, took Scott's plan seriously. Who knew how long the war would last? Lincoln immediately ordered ships to block all Southern ports. At first, the blockade didn't make much difference. Nine out of ten swift cargo boats called "blockade runners" were able to sneak past the big, lumbering warships. However, the blockade gradually became more effective. In the difficult years that would follow, the early decision to block Southern ports would end up making a huge difference. Even the newspapers eventually had to admit it: Old Fuss and Feathers had been right.

Blockades alone, however, would not win the War in the West. Thousands of soldiers would need to be led to the key Confederate forts along important rivers. Who would lead them? Lincoln was known for making surprising picks—both for his Cabinet and for leaders in the military. Often he went against the grain, choosing those in whom he saw a spark or special quality that, perhaps, others did not see. Lincoln saw this kind of spark in a young man named Ulysses S. Grant.

"He is . . . stumpy, unmilitary, slouchy, and Western-looking; very ordinary, in fact," reported one of the lieutenants who served under Grant. "But when he took over, we felt at last that the boss had arrived."

Up until the point at which Grant became "the boss," he had had a rather unremarkable life. Skinny and withdrawn as a child, Grant did not do very well at anything other than caring for horses. He disliked the blood and stench of his father's tannery business. So Jesse Grant encouraged his son's interests and helped him find a career at which he could earn a living.

The older Grant got his son, originally named Hiram Ulysses, into the United States Military Academy at West Point, New York. The Congressman who appointed Grant to the academy, mistakenly put his name on the application as "Ulysses Simpson Grant," Simpson being Grant's mother's maiden name. Although Grant tried to correct his name, officials at the academy told him that it didn't matter what his name was; what mattered was the name on his application. Grant would end up keeping the name "Ulysses S. Grant" for the rest of his life. Because Grant's initials were "U.S.," fellow cadets sometimes called him "Uncle Sam," then simply "Sam."

What followed were more years of failure. Grant never liked West Point and, as a result, graduated in the bottom half of his class. The rules, fancy uniforms, and structured life drove Grant crazy. "A military life has no charms for me," Grant said during his senior year. Still, after graduation he left to serve in the Mexican War, even though he didn't exactly agree with the United States' reasons for fighting.

"I considered my supreme duty was to my flag," Grant would later write. Although he was not thrilled with military life, Grant was entirely devoted to his country. It was a devotion that would never waver.

Married with a young daughter, Grant tried everything to make a living: farming, bill collecting, selling real estate, and even selling firewood on the street corner near his home in Galena, Illinois. Nothing succeeded. Finally, when the Civil War began, Grant rejoined the army and, according to him, never looked back. Because he was one of the few graduates of West Point living in Illinois, he was put in command of a regiment of untrained and undisciplined volunteers. The change in Grant was almost immediate. Friends noticed that he walked taller and seemed totally focused. The men under Grant's command changed, too. Soon, his regiment was winning small battles.

"All he needed was a chance and someone to believe in him," a neighbor said.

In August 1861, President Lincoln believed in Grant enough to promote him to brigadier general of volunteers.

Grant was by no means the picture of an ideal military leader. At five feet seven inches and 134 pounds, he was even smaller than many of the teenage drummer boys. His kind and often shy blue eyes seemed out of place on the battlefield, and his quiet voice and reluctance to order soldiers around made some of his men wonder, at first, if President Lincoln had made a big mistake. But when Grant had something to say, he was both direct and unflinching. And at fighting a war, Grant was far from shy or reluctant.

"The art of war is simple enough," Grant explained to his men. "Find out where your enemy is. Get at him as soon as you can. Strike him as hard as you can, and keep moving on."

Many who had heard of Grant but did not know him personally did not have a very good impression of him. They felt he was reckless in battle, and put his soldiers' lives in danger unnecessarily. It was no secret that Grant drank too much whiskey from time to time, and some worried that his decision-making was blurred by alcohol. However, those who *did* know him personally, knew a man who never drank when leading his men into battle. They knew a man who quietly gained respect and admiration from his soldiers because of his respect for them. And they knew a man who hated war, but loved his country.

"There never was a time," Grant once said when asked if war could be avoided, "when some way could not be found to prevent the drawing of the sword."

And so it was with this love of country and dislike for war that Grant was sent to lead the Union armies in Tennessee in February of 1862.

Fort Donelson was a very important Confederate fort in Tennessee. If Grant and his men could capture it, the route to northern Alabama would be wide open and unguarded by any other forts. Fort Donelson sat facing the Cumberland River, making certain that no Union gunboats could sneak past.

For this very reason, Grant intentionally ordered a small fleet of gunboats to pass directly in front of the fort. As the Rebel soldiers all gathered to defend Donelson and fire on the gunboats, Grant and his regiment of 17,000 men quietly took up positions at the back of the fort, effectively surrounding it.

The Confederates were trapped. As night fell, a rare and bitter snowstorm blew in. The Confederate general, John Floyd, made a bold decision. Because of the heavy snow, John Floyd gambled that the Union guards would not be able to see the Rebels sneaking out of the fort. He was right. As the Union soldiers slept, the Confederates launched a surprise attack. Grant woke to the sound of muskets and shouting.

"Fill your cartridge boxes and get into line!" Grant shouted to his men. "The enemy is trying to escape and must not be permitted to do so!"

General Floyd's men were still surrounded. Though they had managed to surprise Grant's army, they would not escape.

"Come on, you volunteers, come on!" yelled C.F. Smith, one of the commanding officers serving under Grant. "This is your chance! You volunteered to be killed for the love of your country, and now you can be!"

Only minutes after the fighting had begun, General Floyd realized that it would lead to an outright slaughter of his troops if it continued.

Up went the white flag. Perhaps, the Confederates hoped, Grant would at least give them favorable surrender terms. Perhaps he would not take prisoners.

"No terms except an immediate and unconditional surrender can be accepted," Grant replied flatly.

Fort Donelson was the first major victory for the Union. Few lives had been lost, and nearly 13,000 Rebel soldiers had been taken prisoner. Up North, people now cheered the great leadership of Grant and nicknamed him "Unconditional Surrender" Grant. Suddenly, Grant, promoted to major general, was the general everyone in the North loved.

That would soon change.

Six weeks later, Grant and his 42,000 Union troops were working their way through Tennessee and on toward Mississippi. On April 6, the Yankees were camped out at an area named "Pittsburg Landing," but it was more commonly known as "Shiloh" because of the nearby log church of the same name. By all accounts, it was a beautiful spring morning, and the Union soldiers were in good spirits. Many of them were cooking breakfast, polishing their muskets, or writing letters home. There were no plans for battle until the troops reached Mississippi, so everyone was relaxed.

Then, without warning, an army of thousands of Confederate soldiers stormed into the Yankees' camp in a surprise attack.

"The (gun) fire opened—a ripping, roaring, boom bang!" one Confederate remembered. "The air was full of balls and deadly missiles."

The Union soldiers were so shocked and terrified that they dropped whatever they were doing and tore out of the camp. The Rebels then ransacked the tents, picked up abandoned weapons, and even sat down to the breakfasts the Yankees had been preparing.

Quickly, Generals Grant and Sherman tried to regroup, shouting to their fleeing troops to lie flat in a peach orchard and shoot back at the advancing Confederate troops. Other soldiers were ordered to take cover in a sunken wagon road. But in this particular battle, eight out of ten soldiers were fresh recruits who had never seen any fighting. Thousands kept running, throwing their guns down as they went. One new recruit was even seen shooting off his own hand so that he would not have to continue fighting. Still, the majority of soldiers, frightened as they were, remained to fight.

In the area of the sunken road and the orchard, the fighting was so intense that it became known as "the Hornet's Nest." All day long, wave upon wave of men from both sides moved into the Hornet's Nest, and wave after wave of men were shot down.

Finally, as night fell, the battle quieted. But out in the dark fields, the cries of the wounded and dying replaced the sounds of battle.

"At midnight," one Tennessee soldier recalled, "a heavy rain set in. . . . The flashes of lightning revealed the ghastly features of the dead. . . . Oh, what a night of horrors that was!"

Huddled in their camp, a group of Union officers talked quietly. There was no telling just how many soldiers had died, but it had been many thousands. Most of the officers agreed that there was no way the Union could win this battle. Continuing to fight would be madness. It was time to surrender.

Not far away, Grant and Sherman sat staring into a smoky fire. These two generals were close friends who understood each other as well as they understood the horrific game of war.

"Well, Grant, we've had the devil's own day, haven't we?" Sherman finally said.

Grant just nodded calmly and gazed out at the dark fields.

"Yes," he said quietly. "But we'll whip 'em tomorrow."

## CHAPTER 4

"*I* thought I had General Grant just where I wanted him and could finish him up in the morning," the confident Confederate general Beauregard would later write with regret. "Our victory was nearly complete."

But this time, Beauregard would not have the same luck he had had at Bull Run and Fort Sumter. In the middle of the night, another battalion of Union soldiers crept into the tattered Union camp. When morning came, it was Grant who would launch the surprise attack. Beauregard had been certain that the Yankees would not make the first move, and when they did, the Confederates were forced back quickly.

Still, the battle again raged on near the Hornet's Nest until late afternoon. Finally, General Beauregard ordered his overwhelmed troops to retreat. A blood-red sunset fell over the battlefield as Generals Grant and Sherman walked out among the dead, dying, and wounded. They knew the losses had been terrible, but even these two war-hardened leaders were shocked by what they saw.

"It would have been possible," Grant remembered, "to walk across the clearing in any direction, stepping on dead bodies without a foot touching the ground."

For his part, Sherman grimly stated, "The scenes on this field would have cured anyone of war."

Nearly 3,500 men had been killed. Another 16,000 were wounded. When the Battle of Shiloh was fought, it was, by far, the deadliest battle in America's history. In fact, more Americans were killed in the Battle of Shiloh than in the War of 1812 and the Mexican War combined! When news of the losses reached Washington, D.C., many people criticized Grant's leadership.

"He's a maniac and an alcoholic," one senator shouted angrily, believing that Grant should have retreated on the first day. "He should be dismissed immediately."

Others, who had admired Grant only months earlier, now jumped on the bandwagon of criticism and agreed that he must have been drunk during the Battle of Shiloh. President Lincoln waved off these criticisms and rumors with irritation.

So far during the Civil War, Lincoln had often struggled with generals who were too meek and too unwilling to fight. More than a few battles had been lost due to slow-acting or fearful generals. Now, finally, a general of unmatched bravery had won an important battle—only to be rewarded by being accused of drinking.

"Tell me what brand of whiskey Grant drinks," Lincoln responded dryly to these accusations. "I would like to send a barrel of it to my other generals."

Meanwhile, in early spring, the Union army in Washington and the Confederate army near Richmond began gearing up for what would become known as "the Peninsula Campaign." The unusual plan got this name because it involved the Union armies advancing north toward Richmond—from the southern tip of the Virginia peninsula—instead of traveling south from Washington.

Union troops by the thousands would sail south through the Chesapeake Bay and march into ports at the tip of the peninsula. The "Anaconda Plan" didn't seem like such a joke now—because of the blockades, Union ships were able to use the waterways, and Confederate ships were unable to defend the ports. This blocking of the James River was particularly irritating to the Confederates. Not only did it make them vulnerable to Union attacks from the south, it also cut Richmond off from the ocean. News, supplies, and trade were all blocked. The Confederacy had begun the Civil War with practically no navy at all. Aside from lobbing cannonballs at Union ships from riverbanks and shorelines, the Confederates were completely unprepared to wage war on the water. But then a group of Confederate engineers came up with an amazing, if somewhat bizarre, plan: Why not take the hull of an old ship, cover it completely with iron plating, and place a few cannons and heavy guns on each side? In 1862, all ships were made of wood. Something like this iron monster would be able to chug down the river and crash right through the Union's ships, splintering them to bits.

And so the ship was built—or rather it was *rebuilt*. The "old ship" the Confederates started with was the *USS Merrimack*, a warship from the Union navy that the Union had deliberately burned and sunk just before the Battle of Fort Sumter. Use of this ship by the Confederacy was the very thing the Union had tried to avoid.

At 275 feet long, this ship, renamed the *CSS Virginia*, carried about 300 men. Ten guns were positioned at protected openings, and the bow was a huge iron ram, made specifically for puncturing enemy ships. When the North got word of this fearsome new weapon, engineers scrambled to build their own "ironclad," as this type of ship was called, as quickly as possible. Named the *Monitor*, the Union's ironclad began moving slowly—painfully slowly—south from New York, where it had been built, in early March. But before the Monitor could reach the James River, the *Virginia* was lumbering toward an area called Hampton Roads, where ships in the Union blockade patrolled.

"She looked like a giant barn floating on the water," one Union sailor commented. "Or like a huge, half-submerged crocodile."

The Yankees shot round after round of shells and cannonballs at the *Virginia* and watched in horror as the cannonballs bounced right off the iron plates and fell into the water. The monster ship plowed on toward the wooden Union ships.

"All our firing had no more effect than peas from a pop-gun," one officer recalled.

The *Virginia* butted against Union ships as their crews scrambled to shoot furiously at the ironclad. But even as entire stores of ammunition were emptied on the *Virginia*, she moved menacingly through the water, crushing wooden ships and firing her cannons nonstop. After ramming and sinking two of the Union's biggest ships, the *Virginia* and her crew retired for the evening. Nearly 250 Union sailors had been killed; the *Virginia* had lost only two crewmembers. Of course, sailors aboard the *Virginia* suffered ringing in their ears from the deafening noise of cannonballs hitting iron all day.

At daybreak, the *Virginia* headed back to Hampton Roads to try to destroy the few Union vessels that remained in the area. But guarding the wooden ships was something the Confederates had never seen before.

"It looked like an immense shingle floating on the water," one Rebel said, "with a gigantic cheesebox rising from its center."

It was the Union's ironclad, the *Monitor*. She had arrived just in time. What followed was one of the more bizarre "battles" of the war. For several hours, the two iron ships went at it, firing on one another and doing absolutely no damage whatsoever, aside from some dents and scratches. Finally, in frustration, the *Monitor* and the *Virginia* steamed away in opposite directions in a huff. Both sides claimed victory, but nothing had really changed. Union ships still blocked the river, and Confederates sat irritated and helpless on the riverbanks.

In the end, ironclads did not turn out to be very practical. They moved too slowly, were difficult to maneuver, and leaked everywhere. But they were the first step toward a modern navy that would, by the next war, use steel warships. And for a brief twenty-four hours, the second-rate Confederate navy ruled the waters during the Civil War.

Like several other Union generals, George B. McClellan did not move quickly, bravely, or decisively enough to suit Lincoln. At a meeting with some of his generals (McClellan was not in attendance), Lincoln remarked sarcastically, "If General McClellan does not want to use the army, I would like to borrow it for a time." In March 1862, Lincoln removed McClellan from the position of general-in-chief, which he had held for less than five months, and left him commanding only the Army of the Potomac, the Union's main army in the eastern part of the country.

Despite his faults, it was McClellan who was leading the Peninsula Campaign in the spring of 1862. Lincoln had not been happy with the idea of moving up the peninsula. A direct approach from the north made more sense to him, and it would have been faster. In truth, Lincoln believed that McClellan had chosen this approach in order to delay the fighting. Although Lincoln did not have a lot of faith that this particular general had the ability to pull off a somewhat backward attack, McClellan had a great deal of faith in himself. He believed he was, in his words, "the power of the land." He often compared his wisdom and military leadership abilities to those of Napoleon.

"I almost think that were I to win some small success now," McClellan bragged to his wife before heading off to the campaign, "I could become dictator or anything else that might please me—but nothing of that kind would please me—therefore I won't be dictator."

And so with an army of 100,000 men and an ego nearly as large, McClellan headed toward the Virginia peninsula by way of Chesapeake Bay as shouts of "On to Richmond!" once again filled the air. Once on land, the troops moved slowly through the springtime mud, then even more slowly through the marshes. Finally, they came to a complete standstill near Yorktown.

McClellan had suddenly given the order to stop. His face turned pale and an expression of fear crept across it. Not far away, there was an unending thunder of men marching and shouting orders. It sounded as though dozens of military bands were playing, and the rumble of artillery practice filled the air. It was the Confederates—a *lot* of Confederates. McClellan listened with dismay.

"It seems clear that I shall have the whole force of the enemy on my hands," McClellan quickly wrote to Lincoln. "Probably not less than 100,000 men, and probably more."

In fact, an army of barely 30,000 Rebels awaited. Their general, knowing that his men were tremendously outnumbered, used trickery instead of fighting to hold off the enemy. He ordered the troops to make as much noise as possible, to holler and march up and down the road nonstop. All day and night, the racket continued, and it fooled McClellan. Instead of attacking, McClellan ordered his troops to take cover and be quiet.

"You must strike a blow!" Lincoln responded angrily. "You must act!"

But General McClellan refused. He even rudely suggested that if Lincoln thought he could do a better job, he should come down and lead the troops himself. For nearly a month, McClellan stalled, building protective barriers and fretting over attack plans. By the time he finally got up the nerve to order the go-ahead, he discovered that the Confederate troops had already moved up the peninsula closer to Richmond.

"No one but McClellan would have hesitated that long to attack," the Confederate commander laughed.

Now an embarrassed McClellan and his army began pursuing the Confederates up the peninsula. The Yankees won a few skirmishes, but McClellan's stalling had given the Confederates time to reinforce and prepare. Only ten miles outside of Richmond, the Rebels turned so fiercely on the Yankees that McClellan could not continue. His confidence shaken, McClellan was on the verge of giving up. "I am tired of the sickening sight of the battlefield," he complained in a letter to his wife.

This was a critical time for the Confederates. They had to continue to push the Yankees back down the peninsula and away from Richmond, or risk losing the war altogether. Realizing the importance of this push, Confederate President Jefferson Davis appointed his favorite general, Robert E. Lee, to lead the Rebel forces. This appointment renewed McClellan's will to fight. He had heard other Union officers say a lot of negative things about "Bobby" Lee. Lee was considered by many to be an old man. And people thought he was more concerned about his haircut, his moustache, and his uniform than about his troops. People said Lee was soft—that he would be a disaster for the Confederates.

"He is too cautious and weak," McClellan declared happily in another letter home. "He is likely to be timid. Now we will win."

McClellan had been wrong before, and this time he could not have been more wrong.

In a week of ferocious fighting that became known as the Seven Days Battles, Lee and the Confederates pushed the Union army farther and farther away from Richmond. Although the Union actually won most of these battles, it was McClellan, not Lee, who was "too cautious" and failed to regain the ground the Yankees had lost. The casualties during this week were astounding. More than 5,000 soldiers had been killed, and 24,000 were wounded.

The fighting finally came to an end on July 1. Preparing to celebrate the Fourth of July holiday, the soldiers had mixed feelings as they considered how their country, united as one, had fought so hard for independence less than a hundred years earlier. Now Yankees and Rebels were camped across a field from one another. Many were so relieved to be done with the battle that they waved to one another good-naturedly and called back and forth in conversation and even in song. And when Independence Day dawned, the morning sun shone down on a touching scene. As one Confederate private recalled:

> There [were] blackberries in the fields so our boys and the Yanks made a bargain not to fire at each other, and went out in the field . . . and gathered berries together and talked over the fight, and traded tobacco and coffee and newspapers as peacefully and kindly as if we had not been engaged for . . . seven days in butchering one another.

This was a scene that would be played out, in some form or fashion, many times during the Civil War. This was a different kind of war. The soldiers from both sides were from the same country, spoke the same language, and enjoyed the same customs, pastimes, jokes, music, and food. Sometimes it was exceedingly difficult for these young men to make any sense out of killing other young men who were just like themselves.

As the war would grind on, the moments when soldiers from both sides could come together and talk or share simple pleasures would become more and more precious. As one Union man, after a long talk with a Confederate soldier, sadly wrote in a letter home, "We . . . could have settled this war in thirty minutes had it been left to us."

Although the Union had won the bulk of the Seven Days Battles, it didn't really matter—Richmond would remain safe, so it had been a victory for the South. The war would continue. McClellan blamed the Union's loss on the fact that the Confederates had had more soldiers, something that simply was not true.

"If McClellan had a million men," Lincoln's Secretary of War, Edwin Stanton, said in frustration, "he would swear the enemy had two million, and then he would sit down in the mud and yell for three!"

Lincoln hurried down to the peninsula to meet with McClellan. The meeting did not go well at all. Finally, Lincoln ordered McClellan to send his army to join General Pope's army in northern Virginia. This left McClellan without a command, Lincoln simply explaining that he had had enough of McClellan's attitude and his reluctance to be aggressive in battle. But within a few weeks, this changed.

Since the war had begun, the Confederates had been on the defensive. In every battle, from Tennessee to Virginia, they had fought to keep the Yankees out of their territory. But now Robert E. Lee felt that the time had come for the Rebels to attack, not defend. With more than 40,000 soldiers, the general whom McClellan had labeled "timid" was now headed north into Maryland and Pennsylvania.

In Washington, Lincoln anxiously paced his office and met with his advisers. Suddenly, the Confederacy was becoming a real threat, and there was no time to get another general in place. Reluctantly, he turned to McClellan, calling on him to once again command the Army of the Potomac.

"We must use the tools we have," Lincoln explained to his Cabinet. But Lincoln was very worried. The Confederacy had not backed down in the slightest and, in fact, had been winning more battles than the Union. For the tide to turn, the Union needed a victory—a big victory.

As for General McClellan, if he was worried he didn't show it. He happily accepted his old position.

"Again," he said brashly to his wife, "I have been called upon to save the country."

## CHAPTER 5

$\mathcal{W}$ho was Robert E. Lee? In many ways, he was very similar to—and yet the opposite of—his rival, Ulysses S. Grant. Like Grant, he was particularly good with horses when he was a boy. And when he became a young man, he, too, attended West Point. Like Grant, he was never a big fan of war, but he was devoted to his country and also fought in the Mexican War even though he had some misgivings about it. And, like Grant, he would become a famous Civil War general who was loved by his troops and admired by his country.

However, the similarities end there. Lee came from a Virginia family that was both famous and wealthy. His father had fought in the American Revolution and was a close friend of George Washington. Despite his family's wealth, Lee's father often had financial difficulties. And when Robert was only six years old, his father went to the

West Indies to try to recover from a severe beating. From that point on, Lee was raised by his mother. She was very loving and supportive, but her health problems and strained financial situation made it difficult for her to care for her five children. Much responsibility fell to Robert, often the oldest child living at home. Other family members helped them and saw to the children's education, one of those relatives eventually getting Robert an appointment to West Point.

Once at West Point, Lee worked hard to bring pride and happiness to his mother. He was such a perfect student and cadet that his classmates nicknamed him "the Marble Model." During his four years at West Point, Lee did not receive a single demerit, or "black mark" for bad behavior. (Grant, on the other hand, received so many demerits that he was demoted to the rank of "private" for his final year.) In spite of his "perfection," however, Lee was well liked both as a leader and as a kind and generous young man. Unlike Grant, who graduated near the bottom of his class, Lee graduated near the top of his class. And Lee had no struggles after graduation. He was sought after by both the Corps of Engineers and the military, working successfully for years in both.

By the time things started heating up between the North and the South, Lee was considered one of the greatest military leaders in the United States.

The Union wasted no time in offering Lee the top command position of the Northern army. True, he was from Virginia, but Lee often spoke out against the idea of secession, stating that if the South left the Union, the South would ultimately come to ruin. Furthermore, Lee was not quiet about how much he despised slavery. He felt it was a cruel and outdated institution that was an embarrassment to the South. And yet Lee struggled with the idea of leading armies against his native Virginia.

"With all my devotion to the Union and the feeling of loyalty and duty of an American citizen," Lee wrote in a letter to his sister, "I have not been able to make up my mind to raise my hand against my relatives, my children, and my home."

For the year leading up to the Civil War, Lee prayed daily that the troubles between the North and the South would be resolved before they reached the breaking point of war. Abraham Lincoln had personally chosen Lee to be a Union commander, but when the first shots were fired at Fort Sumter and war was declared, Lee reluctantly wrote to Lincoln and explained, "I could not draw my sword on my native state." This was exceedingly difficult for Robert E. Lee, and he promised Lincoln that he would fight only to defend Virginia, not to defeat the Union.

But by the summer of 1862, Lee felt differently. He had seen a lot of war and a tremendous amount of bloodshed, and all of it had been brought about as a result of the North pushing into the South. Now many Southerners wanted to attack Union troops on their own turf. It was time for offense, they argued, not defense. Although Lee had never wanted to be an aggressor against the United States, he now felt he had no choice. Perhaps a surprise defeat of Union troops in their own territory would frighten Northerners into reconsidering whether they wanted to continue this deadly war.

So with his favorite general, Stonewall Jackson, by his side, Lee led his troops north. In contrast to Grant, Lee was the picture of an ideal military leader. His horse, Traveller, was brushed until his coat shone, and a fancy leather saddle with brass stirrups rested upon Traveller's back. Even at the height of summer, Lee was dressed in full uniform, complete with white gloves and a bow tie. His locks of gray hair were neat, and his white beard was trimmed. A tall man, he rode proudly with his head held high.

"General Lee is, almost without exception, the handsomest man of his age I ever saw," a visitor from England once exclaimed. "His manners are most courteous and full of dignity."

When the war began, Lee was 54 and Grant only 39. Lee's age—and his patience on the battlefield—led some people to snicker behind his back and call him "Granny Lee," suggesting that he was too old to lead young soldiers in a war. But his age only endeared him to his admirers, who saw him as a grand and dignified hero. If he had any vices, they were hard to find. He neither swore nor smoked, and about alcohol, Lee explained with a smile, "I like whiskey. I always did, and that is why I never drink it."

Lee's soldiers were entirely devoted to their general, affectionately referring to him as "Uncle Robert" and showing him every respect. And Stonewall Jackson, a man known to distrust and find fault with most military leaders, put his full faith in his commanding general.

"So great is my confidence in General Lee," Jackson once said, "that I am willing to follow him blindfolded."

"It's another Bull Run! Here come the Rebs!"

These were the panicked shouts of Union soldiers as the Rebels once again overtook them on the very same battlefield where the North had suffered a humiliating defeat a year earlier.

For his first battle as he moved north, Lee had devised an unusual plan. Every general knew that it was a very bad idea to divide one's troops; it weakened the advance and broke down communication. No one ever expected a leader to do this intentionally. That was precisely why Lee split his army at the Second Battle of Bull Run.

Stonewall Jackson bravely led only 20,000 men to fight the Union's 60,000 men while Lee waited for just the right moment. As the Yankees used up their ammunition and their energies, the second wave of Confederates bided their time. Jackson's men gave everything they had, terrorizing Union soldiers with their Rebel yells as they charged forward.

"There is nothing like it this side of hell," one Yankee said of the yell. "The peculiar corkscrew sensation that it sends down your backbone cannot be described."

In spite of their yells, however, the Confederates suffered terribly as their outnumbered troops were overwhelmed. Jackson reassured his men, though, as he rode up and down the lines, shouting for them to remain brave and to keep shooting. Meanwhile, on the Union side, a relatively new general, John Pope, had been sent to start this battle, with the promise of McClellan joining him if necessary. But Pope was easily fooled by what he thought was the entire Confederate army, and he brashly sent word that he could handle things on his own.

At the very moment Pope thought he had won the battle, Robert E. Lee sprung the trap. More than 25,000 fresh Confederate soldiers stormed and shouted their way into Bull Run. Making matters worse, the overconfident Pope had sent many of his soldiers back to the camp, because he had been so certain that the Rebels could not win. Now it was the Union that was overwhelmed.

"We were in the very center of hell," one Union soldier recalled. "Men were just filled with bullets, and the fields were full of the dead and dying."

It was a stunning victory for Lee and the Confederates. But, again, the bloodshed was nearly impossible to comprehend. A staggering 25,000 men were reported dead, wounded, or missing. It was the most brutal battle yet in the Civil War, and as soldiers sat around their camps that hot August night, many of them believed that nothing could match what they had witnessed that day. Surely, no battle could be more deadly. As a heavy summer storm moved through, even the booming thunder could not drown out the cries of the many wounded and dying men still lying in the fields. In their tents, many soldiers tossed and turned after an exhausting day of fighting.

"I suppose we sometimes dreaded the mornings after a battle as much as the battle itself," a soldier from Tennessee explained. "It was one thing to kill, but another to tend to the dead."

With every battle, it seemed that the dead piled higher and higher. In the mornings, weary soldiers rode out onto the battlefields with long wagons in which they stacked the bodies six or seven deep. If time allowed, the fallen were buried individually in rows of shallow graves with, perhaps, a small marker. Often, however, long trenches were dug and soldiers were buried without markers or any kind of identification. Perhaps a block of wood quickly engraved to indicate whether the grave held Confederate or Union soldiers was placed nearby, but that was all.

Those doing the burying struggled with what they had to do. In the summer heat, the bodies decayed quickly and then spread disease, so there was no time to identify remains, contact families, and have a proper burial. With every young man who was anonymously placed in a trench, those doing the burying couldn't help but wonder if they would be next.

"I have a horror of being thrown out in a neglected place or [being] trampled on as I have seen a number of graves here," one soldier wrote home after Second Bull Run.

The idea of being hastily buried without a marker in the middle of an empty field hundreds of miles away from home haunted many soldiers more than did the idea of death itself. It was not uncommon for a soldier to head into battle with his name and address written on a small piece of paper that was pinned to the inside of his uniform (a practice that would later lead to the "dog tags" today's soldiers wear). Soldiers hoped against hope that if they were identified, their family would one day return to these distant fields to carry their remains back home.

Perhaps most disturbing of all to a soldier was the fear of his fate if his body was left for the enemy to bury. To the victor went the burial duties. "Don't let the Rebels get me," was the dying request of many a Union soldier, just as "Don't leave me to the Yanks," was a common last gasp of a Confederate. By law and common decency, soldiers were required to bury *all* corpses, regardless of which side they were on. More often than not, this law was followed—but not always.

"It is terribly fearful to think of being killed on the field without a kind hand to hide one's remains from the eye of the world or the gnawing of animals and buzzards," one Confederate wrote in a letter to his wife. As the war progressed and the troops became more exhausted and numb to death itself, bodies of the enemy were sometimes barely covered with dirt. Once, the bodies of seven Union soldiers were thrown down a well by angry and exhausted Confederates. Other times, the corpses of enemy soldiers were simply left where they had fallen. It was not uncommon to see pigs out in the fields eating the remains.

Two years after the Second Battle of Bull Run, troops passed back through the battlefield area. Rains and wind had washed away many of the shallow graves, and bones of the dead stuck up everywhere.

"Bony knees, long toes, and grinning skulls are to be seen in all directions," a soldier reported. "In one place I saw a man's boot protruding from the grave. The boot had rotted, leaving the skeleton toes pointing upward to a land where there is no war."

Robert E. Lee felt a profound sorrow for the number of lives lost at Second Bull Run, but now the war's momentum had shifted to the South. There was no time to waste—the moment had arrived for the Confederates to go on the offensive and continue north. Although Washington was nearby, Lee knew there was no chance of victory there. After Second Bull Run, Union troops flocked to Washington to protect the city and the President.

Instead, Lee became determined to move through Maryland and on into Pennsylvania. It was a very big gamble. Confederate victories in these Northern states could possibly be enough to convince Lincoln to give up the fight for the Union. On the other hand, defeat in the enemy's territory could lead to the final defeat of the Confederacy. It was a gamble that Lee was willing to take.

In the White House, Abraham Lincoln was very worried. With the Union's loss at Second Bull Run, the fear that the Union might actually lose this war became very real. The North *must* win the next battle.

Furthermore, Lincoln had a very important announcement he wanted to make: He intended to free all slaves in the Confederate states. Not only was freeing the slaves the right thing to do, it would also strike a blow to the South. Still, Lincoln and his Cabinet knew that the Union had to win a decisive victory first. Otherwise, the act of freeing slaves would look like a desperate move by the losing side.

And Lincoln worried about General McClellan. McClellan was now leading the army that was in pursuit of Lee, and time was of the essence. If Lee got too far ahead and had more time to organize and plan, the Union troops would be in a lot of trouble once they caught up. Lincoln had ordered McClellan to move quickly, but in his typical fashion, McClellan was moving slowly and cautiously.

This is what Robert E. Lee had been banking on. Once again, he split up his troops, sending Stonewall Jackson and 20,000 men to quickly seize the arsenal at Harper's Ferry in order to replenish the army's weapons. Meanwhile, Lee and 18,000 soldiers headed north. McClellan plodded along with his troops and sent terse messages back to the President, assuring him that everything was under control. But in reality, McClellan had no idea where Lee and the Rebels were or what they were doing.

Then a one-in-a-million opportunity fell right into McClellan's hands.

"Sir, we found this along the road," two of McClellan's soldiers said, handing him a strange package. "We think it might be important."

The general looked at it and frowned. It was simply a piece of paper wrapped around three cigars. But as McClellan unwrapped the paper, he saw that it was a map with instructions. It was Lee's secret battle plan! Some careless officer had dropped the package when the Confederate troops had passed by two days earlier. McClellan laughed out loud at this unbelievable piece of luck.

"Here is a paper with which, if I cannot whip Bobby Lee, I will be willing to go home," McClellan said with a gleam in his eyes. "Quickly, now—we must catch them at their own game."

## CHAPTER 6

"*I* have never seen such a mass of filthy, strong-smelling men," a resident of Frederick, Maryland, declared as he watched the Confederates march past one morning in September. "Scratching all the time, they must have been covered in fleas and who knows what else."

"They were the dirtiest I ever saw," claimed another Maryland resident. "A most ragged, lean, and hungry set of wolves. Yet there was a dash about them that the Northern men lacked."

Robert E. Lee knew that his Army of Northern Virginia, as it was named, did not look very impressive. Few of the men actually owned uniforms; most were dressed in tattered farm clothes. Half of Lee's men marched barefoot, and nearly all the men were unshaven, dusty, and carrying rusty rifles. Still, Lee hoped that the "dash" of his soldiers would impress the Marylanders as the Rebels passed through. After all, these were the men who had beaten the Yankees again and again.

Because Maryland was a border state, Lee and Confederate president, Jefferson Davis, hoped that those who lived there might be swayed to join the South. If Maryland also seceded, Washington, D.C., would be surrounded. It would be a major advantage for the Confederates. So, as the men marched through, they sang "Maryland, My Maryland" and smiled and waved at townspeople. But news of the war's horrifying battles had reached even the smallest towns. Nearly everyone ran to lock doors and hide in back rooms until the soldiers had passed through.

Miles behind, General McClellan bragged in a wire to Lincoln, "I have all the plans of the Rebels, and will catch them in their own trap. Will send you trophies."

Still, McClellan stalled for a critical sixteen hours, again fretting over the size of the enemy's army. In fact, Lee had only 18,000 soldiers to McClellan's 75,000, but as McClellan wasted time, General Stonewall Jackson and General James Longstreet— with their armies—were on their way to join up with Lee. Finally, on the afternoon of September 16, the Union forces approached Sharpsburg, Maryland, near a creek named Antietam.

"Their number increased, and larger and larger grew the field of blue," a Confederate soldier remembered, "until it seemed to stretch as far as the eye could see. From the tops of the mountains down to the edges of the stream gathered the great army of McClellan."

McClellan may have been leading an impressive army, but he fell back on his same old bad habits. Instead of attacking immediately, McClellan waited until the morning, giving Lee and Jackson that much more time to gather their troops and arrange battle plans. That night, sniper fire echoed through the farm valley, shouts and drumbeats flared up, and every soldier knew that the next day would bring terror, pain, and maybe death. Very late that night, a Union general lay awake listening to all the pre-battle restlessness.

"The night was so dark, so obscure, so mysterious, and so uncertain," he later wrote. "A great battle was coming—one that might decide the fate of our country."

The Battle of Antietam, named for the nearby creek, began as the first rays of sunlight drifted through the morning fog on September 17, 1862. The daylong battle was really three separate battles fought one after another in three different locations. The first one, fought in the morning, took place in and near a cornfield. It was, as many soldiers described it, a scene of outright slaughter. The two sides advanced on one another in a rush. Both the Rebels and Yankees were in a frenzy to win quickly, and they fired their guns nonstop. So many bullets filled the air that within an hour, the entire field of cornstalks had been flattened, leaving soldiers nowhere to hide. Wave after wave of men ran out into the stripped cornfield, shooting wildly into the smoke and dust. Almost instantly, they fell to the ground.

"The slain lay in rows precisely as they had stood in their ranks a few minutes before," a Union general later commented sadly.

By barely 9:00 in the morning, 8,000 soldiers had been killed or wounded. Because of the intensity of the fighting, McClellan still believed he was outnumbered, but Generals Lee and Jackson knew that, in fact, the Confederates were outnumbered by more than 40,000 Union soldiers.

"For God's sake," Jackson was heard shouting above the roar of gunfire, "We must get out of this! Move back, boys!"

Thousands of Rebel troops moved from the cornfield and repositioned themselves along an old dirt road. The road had been used for so long by so many heavy farm wagons that it was now sunken several feet. As the Yankee troops pursued the enemy, orders were given to the Confederates in the sunken road to lie low and remain quiet. Hidden from the Union troops' sight, the Rebels aimed their guns and waited silently for a sign from their commanding officers.

"Soon the Yankees were so close that we might have seen the eagles on their buttons," one soldier recalled.

With the shout of "Now!" the Confederates fired on the surprised Union soldiers. In a flash, the entire frontline of Union soldiers went down. Another regiment was sent in, and another fell. This happened again and again. Finally, a group of New York soldiers managed to climb up a small hill where they were able to shoot down directly into the sunken road. Now the Confederates were trapped.

"We were shooting them like sheep in a pen," a Union soldier later said. "Not one man in there had a chance in hell." So many men were shot in the road that they lay three and four bodies deep, and the sunken road would become remembered as Bloody Lane.

The Confederates were more successful in keeping Union forces from crossing Antietam Creek. McClellan had ordered Burnside to lead his troops across the creek in order to attack the village of Sharpsburg. However, Burnside had infuriated McClellan by dawdling—waiting hours before he followed the order. When Burnside finally *did* try to cross, he led his army across an old stone bridge, which would become known as "Burnside's Bridge," rather than wading across the creek in a lightly defended shallow area. A bottleneck developed on the bridge, enabling 400 Confederates, many of them firing from protected places, to hold off 12,500 Union soldiers for about three hours—enough time for reinforcements to arrive.

Finally, the Yankees broke the Confederates, and the Rebels turned and ran.

"Oh, how I ran!" one soldier said. "I was afraid of being struck in the *back*, and I frequently turned around in running, so as to avoid if possible so disgraceful a wound."

At the end of the day, the armies stood almost exactly where they had stood at dawn. Each had held its ground—Lee risking everything to do so, and McClellan, as usual, holding armies in reserve.

It had been the bloodiest day of the Civil War so far. More than 12,000 Union soldiers were dead, wounded, or missing. And while the Confederates suffered slightly fewer casualties, the nearly 11,000 lost represented nearly a third of the entire Confederate Army of Northern Virginia. Lee's important army had never been weaker.

"God bless you and all with you," Lincoln wired to McClellan. "Destroy the Rebel army, if possible."

Lincoln knew, as did the Confederates and most of McClellan's men, that if the Union kept pursuing what was left of Lee's army, the war would be over. Without the Army of Northern Virginia, the Confederate capital in Richmond would have no defense. If Richmond could be taken, the North would be the victor. It was as simple as that.

Yet, amazingly, McClellan once again did nothing. As dawn broke the next morning, Lee's limping army quietly slipped out of sight and headed back to Virginia. And McClellan willingly allowed it. As a result of this inexplicable lack of action, the war would continue for nearly three more years. Thousands more would die, and many more battles would be fought—some even bloodier than Antietam.

The wounded "filled every building and overflowed into the countryside," a Maryland farmer recalled after the Battle of Antietam. "They filled farmhouses, barns, corncribs, cabins—wherever four walls and a roof were found together."

It is difficult to imagine the peaceful little town of Sharpsburg, Maryland, with its population of 1,300, dealing with 23,000 victims of war after the Battle of Antietam. The dead and wounded soldiers blocked roads, covered fields, and lined creek banks. The few permanent hospitals at that time were so far away that taking the wounded to them was impractical if not impossible. There were no painkillers to give to horribly injured soldiers while they awaited care, and, worst of all, the doctors and surgeons who tended to the soldiers had very little understanding of medicine.

"If a fellow has to go to the hospital, you might as well say goodbye," one Union soldier commented after Antietam, and most soldiers would have agreed with that statement.

The Civil War was tragically unique in that it was a war in which modern weapons were used, but modern methods of fighting—and modern medicine—were not. Prior to the 1860s, soldiers had used awkward, slow-loading muskets that were accurate only when shot within fifty yards of their target. This meant that when opposing sides charged into battle, they needed to get very close to one another to do any kind of damage.

But now a new rifle was being utilized. The spiral grooves in the gun barrel sent a bullet spinning accurately toward its target—and a good marksman with time to aim could hit a man-sized target 500 yards away.

In addition, the new rifle used a new bullet called a "Minié ball" (pronounced "minnie ball"), named after its inventor, C.E. Minié. The Minié ball was a hollow soft-lead bullet that was quick and easy to load. It was a .58 caliber bullet, meaning that it was more than one-half inch in diameter. It could pulverize tissue and turn a man's thigh bone into a hundred fragments. Soldiers struck in the torso with a Minié ball nearly always died, as the bullets destroyed their internal organs. It was not uncommon to see soldiers dead on the battlefield with their shirts pulled up. It was believed that many men were checking to see where they had been hit. If their torso had been struck, the soldiers knew they had better prepare to die.

Making matters worse, military leaders of the day were used to the old head-to-head charges, and they continued to order their troops to wait to attack until the enemy was within fifty to one hundred feet. Soldiers who were fired upon at a distance of fifty feet were nearly always killed or seriously wounded. This mistake of getting too close to the enemy is what led, in large part, to the appalling number of deaths and injuries on the battlefields. It is estimated that ninety percent of battle casualties resulted from the new rifle and the destructive Minié ball.

And those who survived being shot braced themselves for a horror nearly as dreadful as the battlefield: the hospital. A field hospital was not much more than a dirty tent with a few cots, some rolls of bandaging, and a bloody surgery table made by placing a board between two water kegs. There was no boiling water, soap, or any kind of disinfectant to be found, and doctors rarely washed their hands between treating one patient and treating another. Today, this seems appalling, but in the 1860s, germs had yet to be discovered. And because no one had any idea what germs were, no one realized that these medical practices could lead to infection.

But it wasn't infection that soldiers feared—it was amputation. Because the new guns and bullets shattered bones beyond repair, doctors could do no more than chop off limbs at the point where the bullet had struck. And while doctors didn't understand infection, they knew that flesh would rot if a bullet wound was not taken care of quickly. As a result, most field hospitals looked like amputation assembly lines.

"A large hole was dug in the yard, about the size of a small cellar," one soldier remembered, "and into this the legs and arms were thrown as they were lopped off by surgeons. In a house nearby that was being used as a hospital, we watched arms and feet being tossed out the windows all day."

The surgeons used what looked more like carpenter's tools than surgical instruments. A wounded man was put to sleep with chloroform or whiskey, and then hammers, picks, and a large saw were used to cut off the shattered limb. (On rare occasions when there was no chloroform or whiskey, soldiers were simply given a bullet to bite down on while enduring the pain. This is where the phrase "bite the bullet" came from.) After the amputation, a doctor did little more than wipe the blade of the saw on his apron, shake the blood off his hands, and call for the next patient.

Nonetheless, amputations really did save lives, and though Civil War surgeons were often referred to as butchers, they did the best they could do. It was those mysterious germs that killed far more soldiers. In fact, throughout the Civil War, nearly twice as many men died from disease as from battle. It seems hard to imagine today, but in the 1860s no one thought there was anything wrong with serving three-day-old food that had not been kept cold or, worse yet, digging a latrine right next to the camp's water supply.

When entire camps or hospitals of soldiers became sick with dysentery or typhoid, doctors scratched their heads in puzzlement. The connection between unsanitary conditions and disease would not be made for another decade. Meanwhile, treatments for disease ranged from cutting patients open to "bleed" the disease out of them, to giving the men a remedy of honey mixed with turpentine, strychnine, or mercury—all three of which were poisonous. When soldiers' teeth fell out and they became delirious from the poison, doctors scratched their heads again.

"The big battles ain't as bad as the big fevers," a frightened and sick drummer boy wrote home to his parents. "I know I am awful brave, but sometimes I reckon I miss my mother."

Often, the only comfort to a sick, wounded, or dying man was the kindness of a nurse. In past wars, wounded soldiers had been treated by men in the military medical corps. But as the war progressed and more and more men were needed for fighting, women were called upon to help care for the wounded. Most female nurses performed the everyday (if gruesome and sometimes heartbreaking) tasks of cleaning wounds, changing dressings, and writing last letters home for dying men. However, some nurses went far beyond the call of duty. One such nurse was Clara Barton.

Barton was not satisfied with waiting for the wounded to come to her—she went to the wounded. In the battles of both Second Bull Run and Antietam, Barton walked out onto the fields amid flying bullets and tended to the injured. She carried water, bandages, and sometimes even whiskey to help ease the pain of the hurt soldiers. Some men claimed that when they saw Barton kneel down next to them in her dark skirt, bonnet, and bright red bow, they believed she was an angel. Thus, the "Angel of the Battlefield," as she was often called, risked her own life again and again to save others.

In the cornfield battle at Antietam, Barton held the head of a wounded man in her lap as she tried to give him water. Suddenly, as she lifted her arm to support him, she felt a twitch in the sleeve of her dress.

"A bullet had passed between my body and the right arm which supported him, cutting through my sleeve and passing through his chest," Barton would later write. The soldier immediately died in her arms.

As early on as 1862, Barton had already grown frustrated with how poorly soldiers were often cared for. On her own, she oversaw the establishment of field hospitals at several battle sites. And, not content with hospitals alone, Barton organized a private relief agency to help sick and wounded soldiers. One hundred and fifty years later, this agency—the American Red Cross—is still hard at work.

And so it was, on the cool, misty morning of September 18, 1862, that Clara Barton walked out onto the battlefields to help retrieve both the dead and the wounded. The task before her and before those soldiers chosen for this particularly dreadful job seemed impossible. All day and into the night, injured men were carried to a farm, where they waited, often in agony, for medical attention.

"The men were brought down from the field," Barton wrote, "till they covered acres. By midnight there must have been three thousand helpless men lying in the hay."

Barton worked for nearly three days without sleep until she collapsed from exhaustion and the beginnings of typhoid fever. However, even as a supply wagon carried her back to Washington, where she would regain her strength, Barton was making plans to return to the battlefields of the Civil War.

Meanwhile, General McClellan scoffed at those who condemned his hesitation and lack of action at

Antietam. After all, McClellan thought, the Union had won this battle. McClellan believed he should be regarded as a hero!

But not everyone agreed.

"In my estimation," commented the head Union surgeon at Antietam, "General McClellan, with all his laurels, sinks into insignificance beside the true heroine of the age, the Angel of the Battlefield."

# CHAPTER 7

*A*braham Lincoln looked tired. Many people thought he looked as though he had aged ten years in the eighteen months since the United States had been divided by war. There were few people who wanted this war to end more than Lincoln did, and just when the Confederates were within grasp, McClellan had stalled yet again.

"I said I would remove him if he let Lee's army get away from him," Lincoln reminded his favorite advisor, "and I must do so. General McClellan has got a case of the 'slows.'"

As for McClellan, he was stunned when he received word of being removed from command. "It is a great mistake," he complained bitterly. "Alas for my poor country!"

The Union's performance at Antietam was far from the convincing win that Lincoln had wanted, but it would have to do. The President had made a promise, and he would keep it.

"I wish that we were in a better condition," Lincoln said to his Cabinet. "But I think the time has come."

Only five days after the Battle of Antietam, Lincoln sent out a warning to the Confederate States of America. If these states did not agree to lay down their weapons and return to the Union by January 1, 1863, all their slaves would be set "forever free."

Known as the Emancipation (meaning "freedom") Proclamation, this bold decision surprised abolitionists as well as slave owners. Lincoln knew exactly how important this decision was.

"If my name ever goes into history," Lincoln said, "it will be for this act."

However, many Southerners laughed out loud at Lincoln's proclamation. Jefferson Davis waved it off as ridiculous, asking how the president of a different country planned to enforce his new law where he had no power. Furthermore, Davis and many Southerners angrily demanded to know what Lincoln planned to do about the slaves in the North and in the border states. If Lincoln was so dead-set on freeing slaves, why not free them everywhere?

In fact, while Lincoln was personally against slavery, he was more concerned about saving the Union than about the emancipation of blacks.

"If I could save the Union without freeing any slave I would do it," Lincoln once admitted, "and if I could save it by freeing all the slaves I would do it; and if I could save it by freeing some and leaving others alone I would also do that."

Now Lincoln had decided to free slaves in the states that had seceded from the Union and leave the others alone. He knew that this would change the war in some very important ways. For one thing, it would give Union armies something new and real to fight for: the liberation of people unfairly held in bondage. In addition, by the end of 1862, many Union soldiers were losing their desire to fight; the war no longer seemed exciting or important. Many were not even sure why they were fighting at all.

"If the South hates the North so damn much," a New York soldier complained, "why not just let them have their own country and let us stop dying over it?"

Southern troops, on the other hand, knew *exactly* why they were fighting. Defending their homes and families was a point of pride and an absolute necessity. It was a much more personal war for the Rebels, and this was why, Lincoln believed, the South continued to win battles against all odds. Outnumbered, poorly armed, half-starved, and dressed in rags, the Rebel troops nonetheless continued to push on. Now Lincoln hoped that the exhilaration of bringing freedom to millions of people throughout the South would inspire Union troops to fight even harder.

But there was another very important reason for Lincoln's announcement. A 1792 law had officially denied blacks the right to become soldiers. However, President Lincoln let it be known that once the Emancipation Proclamation took effect, African Americans would be encouraged to join Union forces. Many black men could barely wait to sign up.

"I will draw my sword against my oppressor and the oppressors of my race," a freed slave living in Pennsylvania said, echoing the feelings of many black men. "I will sacrifice everything in order to save the gift of freedom for my race."

One former slave, Frederick Douglass, was particularly excited about the opportunity for blacks to fight. As a young boy, Douglass had risked his life just to learn how to read and write. Even as a child, Douglass knew that learning must be very important if white men were so determined to keep slaves totally uneducated. Once he had learned to read, Frederick Douglass read everything he could get his hands on—and the world opened up to him. Unfortunately, it was a world that was hostile to slaves.

"I didn't know I was a slave," Douglass would later write, "until I found out I couldn't do the things I wanted."

Once Frederick Douglass discovered all the things he was *not* allowed to do, he became determined to escape slavery and do all those things and more. In time, Douglass would not only successfully run away from his owner, he would also become a famous writer, speaker, and abolitionist. His ideas were decades ahead of his time. He spoke out for the rights of women, Native Americans, and immigrants, believing that all human beings, without exception, deserved equal treatment. Douglass often said, "I would unite with anybody to do right and with nobody to do wrong."

Douglass had long argued that all free black people should have the right to become United States citizens. While this had not yet happened, Douglass saw that being allowed to fight in the Civil War alongside white men was a major step toward citizenship.

"Let the black man get upon his person the brass letters, *U.S.*," Douglass said in a speech, "let him get an eagle on his button, and a musket on his shoulder and bullets in his pocket, and there is no power on earth or under the earth which can deny that he has earned the right of citizenship in the United States."

As expected, slave owners in the South were furious with the idea of the black man having a musket on his shoulder. More specifically, slave owners were terrified. In some areas of the Deep

South, slaves outnumbered whites. Many people believed that if slaves actually took up arms and fought for the North, plantation owners and their families would be in great danger. In desperation, slaveholders made up outrageous stories about the Yankees in an attempt to scare their slaves away from joining Union forces.

"They plan to sign you on to fight and then kill all of you when they have won" was a popular scare tactic. More commonly, though, slave owners simply pointed out that the slaves would have nowhere to go, no home, and no chance of survival if they left the plantation.

What the slave owners failed to understand, however, was that freedom was far more important to their slaves than anything else was. No threats or lies could fool black people into believing that bondage was better than liberty. So, throughout the South, millions of African Americans waited impatiently for New Year's Day, 1863.

"We were waiting and listening as for a bolt from the sky," Frederick Douglass wrote of the anticipation. "We were watching . . . by the dim light of the stars for the dawn of a new day . . . we were longing for the answer to the agonizing prayers of centuries."

Some, including Douglass, were not entirely convinced that Lincoln would actually sign the Emancipation Proclamation when New Year's Day rolled around. Douglass had often complained that Lincoln had not moved quickly enough to free the slaves. Others felt that Lincoln was only threatening to free slaves to scare the Confederates. Would Lincoln really keep his promise?

On New Year's Day, black people gathered in churches throughout the North and South waiting for the news. At the White House in Washington, Lincoln held a large party that went on for hours. He shook so many hands that day that his own hand was shaking as he walked to his office that night to sign the Proclamation.

"If my hand trembles as I sign my name, people will say that I was afraid," Lincoln said to aides and Cabinet members standing around him.

"But you are not afraid, are you, Mr. President?" one young aide asked.

Lincoln smiled. "No. I am not afraid," he said quietly. And with that, he signed the document that freed more than four million black men, women, and children.

"Who would be free themselves must strike the blow," Frederick Douglass said in a speech to rally black Union soldiers in 1863. "This is your golden opportunity!"

During the next two years of the Civil War, nearly 200,000 African Americans would willingly fight for the Union cause. However, these soldiers were not treated as equals to white soldiers. They were paid less and were seldom allowed to become officers. Black troops were separated from white troops, and they were typically used for labor jobs such as cooking, burial detail, and guard duty rather than for combat.

Even in the North, it was widely believed that black men had neither the bravery nor the skill to enter the battlefield. Although people in the Union typically did not agree with slavery, most still felt that black and white people were quite different and that white people were generally superior to blacks. In the 1860s, this was not viewed as racism; it was simply the attitude of that era. It would be many decades before that attitude would change. Nonetheless, young black men began to wonder if this "golden opportunity" Douglass spoke about was really an opportunity at all. How could they prove themselves if they never got the chance?

Then in July of 1863, the opportunity arrived. A regiment of black soldiers, the 54th Massachusetts Volunteer Infantry, was sent to South Carolina after their white commander, Colonel Robert Shaw, had insisted that his men were just as brave as any white soldiers. Again and again, Shaw had been turned down, told that black men wouldn't be brave enough to fight. But now Shaw and the 54th Massachusetts were being given a chance—and facing a terribly dangerous battle. Near Charleston, on Morris Island, sat a well-guarded fort named Fort Wagner. Only a week earlier, a Union battalion of white soldiers had quickly given up when it appeared they couldn't win. Attacking Fort Wagner was exceedingly tricky. Because it had the Atlantic Ocean to the east and swamps to the west, the only possible line of attack was directly into Confederate guns.

Colonel Shaw explained the perils to his men. Clearly there would be bloodshed and death. Not one of the men flinched. Instead, they raised the battle cry "Come on, 54th!" in a thundering cheer.

On the evening of July 18, the 54th Massachusetts marched head-on into Confederate fire. The Confederates were certainly outnumbered, but they were completely protected within the fort. Realistically, there was no way Shaw's men could win. This was the first battle any of these young men of the 54th had experienced, but even in the face of impossible odds, they refused to retreat. Hundreds of black soldiers fell to the sand, but still they pushed on. Then, amazingly, a group of men from the 54th was able to storm the fort and get inside. For over an hour, these Union soldiers fought the Rebels in hand-to-hand combat.

However, in spite of the bravery of the 54th Massachusetts, the protected Fort Wagner proved to be too much. Colonel Shaw's last words were the rallying "Come on, 54th!" moments before he was shot through the heart and killed. Following the battle, the Confederates threw Shaw's body into a pit with the bodies of his black soldiers who had also been killed. They thought this was the ultimate insult and wrote a letter to Shaw's father scoffing, "We buried him with his niggers."

However, Shaw's father thought just the opposite. In his mind, what the Confederates had done had been an honor:

"We can imagine no holier place than that in which he lies, among his brave and devoted followers, nor wish for him better company," his father wrote back. "What a bodyguard he has!"

In the North, news of the valor of the 54th Massachusetts was a headline in every newspaper and the topic of every conversation. The battle may have been a loss, but it was a very honorable loss. It changed the way blacks would participate in the Civil War, and it changed the minds of those who had doubted the bravery of African Americans. And in the South, freed slaves celebrated the now-famous fierceness of their Northern brothers by rushing to Union bases throughout the South and joining the Union army. After watching a battalion of black volunteers, a Union officer wrote home to his wife: "I never would have believed that a common plantation Negro could be brought to face a white man. I supposed that everything in the shape of spirit and self-respect had been crushed out of them generations back. I am glad to find myself mistaken."

Confederates were both furious and frightened. Already far outnumbered by Union forces, Southerners worried that the addition of black soldiers could be the last straw. Some slave owners refused to let their slaves leave, threatening to kill them if they tried. But in other areas, Union soldiers protected slaves as they walked away from the plantations, often singing and shouting in celebration. And owners could do nothing but watch in frustration.

"Now I believe we *could* lose this war," wrote a cotton plantation owner in Alabama. "Damn Lincoln and his Proclamation! Two hundred of my slaves went to the Yankees today."

Some Rebels responded by focusing on killing as many black men as possible. Black soldiers who were taken as prisoners were often either tortured or forced back into slavery. In one particularly gruesome incident, nearly 300 African-American soldiers were slaughtered after they had laid down their arms and surrendered in a battle at Fort Pillow. The Confederate officer who ordered the massacre, General Nathan Bedford Forrest, bragged and exaggerated about what would later be considered a war crime.

"The [Mississippi] river," Forrest said, "was dyed with the blood of the slaughtered for two hundred yards. The approximate loss was upward of five hundred killed . . . My loss was only about twenty killed. It is hoped that these facts will demonstrate to the Northern people that Negro soldiers cannot cope with Southerners."

But black soldiers did "cope with Southerners." Because they knew the consequences if they were captured, they often fought more fiercely than white soldiers. Furthermore, the cause of freedom was certainly more personal and immediate to black soldiers. One young freed slave named Samuel joined the Union forces, hoping that once the war was won, he would be reunited with his wife. A year earlier she and Samuel had been separated when she was sold to a different plantation. Even as Samuel fought, his wife continued to be enslaved by a plantation owner who refused to let her leave.

"Great is the outpouring of the colored people that is now rallying with the hearts of lions against that very curse that has separated you and me," Samuel wrote to his young wife. "Yet we shall meet again . . . and oh what a happy time that will be."

# CHAPTER 8

*I*t was no secret that President Lincoln had had difficulty finding a suitable commander for the Army of the Potomac. He had already removed McClellan once. Now, because McClellan had failed yet again to pursue the Confederate army and soundly defeat it, Lincoln removed him again. He told one of his aides, "For organizing an army, for preparing an army for the field, or for fighting a defensive campaign, I will back General McClellan against any general of modern times—I don't know but of ancient times also. But I begin to feel as if he would never get ready to fight!"

To replace McClellan, Lincoln chose a general who had refused the command twice before: Ambrose Burnside. Although Burnside did not consider himself qualified for the position, Lincoln had faith in him. In addition, Burnside was popular with his soldiers, and Lincoln was betting on this close relationship to inspire the Yankees to victory. Besides, this time Lincoln was *ordering* Burnside to take the command.

And so it was, that near Fredericksburg, Virginia, Robert E. Lee would face yet another Union general. Ambrose Burnside was a smart man with both a sense of humor and a sense of humility. He was tall and nearly bald, but he made up for the lack of hair on his head with a thick moustache that appeared to extend all the way to his ears (the term "sideburns" would come from a play on Burnside's name). He was a natural leader and was deeply dedicated to the Union's cause. However, Ambrose Burnside lacked confidence. This was something that Ulysses S. Grant had noticed the first time he had met Burnside. Although Grant had warned Lincoln about this, Lincoln was running out of generals. Burnside would have to do.

In spite of his lack of faith in himself, Burnside put together an unusual, but good, battle plan. He would use pontoon bridges (floating bridges) to get his army across the Rappahannock River, and then the soldiers would march south to Richmond. Burnside knew that if he moved quickly, there was no way Lee's army could catch the Army of the Potomac. And, unlike McClellan, Burnside was ready to act.

However, this time it was the Union War Department that dropped the ball. The pontoons were delayed for more than eight days, and during that time, Lee and Stonewall Jackson figured out what Burnside was up to. Lee moved 75,000 men to the hillsides and bluffs overlooking open fields near where he believed Burnside's 115,000 troops were camped, hidden along the river. Lee was uneasy. He knew that Burnside was well aware that Confederate troops now filled the hillsides. Certainly, Burnside and the Yankees had heard the Rebel troops moving into position. So how would Burnside attack now? What would his approach be?

"The enemy will be more surprised by a crossing immediately in front of them," Burnside decided.

There was, perhaps, no one more surprised than Robert E. Lee as he watched the Army of the Potomac stream out into the valley below. Burnside had made an astonishingly bad decision. Now his men would have to charge more than half a mile across an open field that was entirely surrounded by Confederates. And nearly every Confederate soldier had his rifle aimed at the men running across the field.

"It was murder, not warfare," one Confederate recalled. "A chicken could not live on that field when we opened fire on it."

The Union suffered nearly 13,000 casualties that day as line after line of brave Yankees charged across the field, their gleaming bayonets in front of them, and their voices raised in a roar. Robert E.

Lee watched from his perch. He found no joy in seeing soldiers fall in such great numbers, even if they were the enemy.

"It is well that war is so terrible," he was heard to remark grimly as he turned away from the slaughter. "Otherwise, we should grow too fond of it."

Burnside had been right—he had not been ready to lead the Union army to Richmond. In horror, he ordered his troops to retreat. That night, temperatures fell into the teens. The injured lying in the bloody field slowly froze to death, many of them crying out for help half the night. Burnside, frantic with regret and sorrow, offered to personally lead a fresh attack in the morning. But his gathered officers just shook their heads.

"That would be suicide, sir," one remarked. "We've seen enough death today."

So, once again, the Army of the Potomac returned to Washington, and Richmond remained strongly protected by Lee and Stonewall Jackson. When the news of the terrible defeat at the Battle of Fredericksburg reached Lincoln, he slumped over his desk and held his head in his hands.

"If there is a worse place than hell," Lincoln exclaimed, "I am in it."

In April, 1863, Lincoln would put yet another general in charge of the Army of the Potomac. The new man, "Fighting" Joe Hooker, was known to be quick-acting and brutal. And he was confident. In fact, Lincoln, a man known to admire humility, sometimes worried that his new general might be *too* confident.

"May God have mercy on General Lee," Hooker said as he prepared to lead his army toward Richmond, "for I will have none."

Not far from the town of Chancellorsville, Virginia, General Hooker set a trap by placing his men on either side of a spot that he guessed Lee's army would pass. Hooker guessed right. His army of 130,000 surrounded Lee's 60,000 men. Finally, it looked as though the Union would have a strong victory. Clearly, Hooker thought, Lee had no choice but to surrender and retreat. He would not be able to fight his way out of this one.

Then again the unexpected happened. Instead of retreating, Lee's army attacked suddenly and violently. With Stonewall Jackson leading one flank and Lee leading another, they charged into the Union camps.

"It was a perfect whirlwind of men," one Union soldier wrote in a letter. "The enemy seemed to come from every direction."

Hooker was so shocked that he was unable to act. His confidence shattered into a million pieces. Some of his soldiers described him as looking like a rabbit frozen with fear in front of a fox. As Lee and Jackson repeatedly changed directions and confused the Yankees, General Hooker stood, nearly motionless, on the porch of a house that overlooked the battle. Finally, a Confederate shell shot a piece of the porch's roof off, and Hooker was hit on the head and knocked out. He regained consciousness an hour or so later, but remained in a fog of confusion.

What had been a nightmare of ice and cold in Fredericksburg was now a terror of fire in Chancellorsville. The ground was dry and covered with leaves. Exploding shells soon caught an entire area known as "the Wilderness" on fire, and terrified soldiers scattered. Hundreds of injured soldiers were burned alive, unable to crawl out of the quickly burning Wilderness. For many soldiers, the sights and sounds of this fire haunted them more than any other gruesome incident of the entire Civil War.

The Battle of Chancellorsville was Robert E. Lee's high point and his greatest victory. But with it came 13,000 casualties for the Army of Northern Virginia. Because so many soldiers had already been killed, injured, or captured in previous battles, this number again represented a substantial percentage of Lee's remaining army. This was a loss the Confederates would not recover from.

Perhaps the greatest loss to Lee personally, however, was that of his friend and trusted general,

Stonewall Jackson. Struck by friendly fire, Jackson had to have his left arm amputated.

"He has lost his left arm," Lee said sadly, "but I have lost my right arm."

The leader who had been Lee's right-hand man for two years now lay in a hospital bed. Infection set in, then pneumonia, and within days, Jackson was on the brink of death. Slipping in and out of consciousness, Stonewall Jackson seemed to be fighting a battle to the very end. In his final moments, he cried out, "Prepare for battle! Pass the infantry to the front!"

Then, slowly, a relieved smile spread over General Jackson's face, and he spoke his last words: "Let us cross over the river, and rest under the shade of the trees."

"Vicksburg is the key," Abraham Lincoln said of Vicksburg, Mississippi. "The war can never be brought to a close until the key is in our pocket."

Things were not going well at all for the Union in Virginia. Lincoln began to feel as though all of his generals were doomed—except for one. Ulysses S. Grant continued to have moderate success in the War in the West. Now, in early 1863, the last strong point along the Mississippi River that had not been captured by the Union was the city of Vicksburg.

As a young man, Lincoln had worked as a flatboat operator along the Mississippi. He knew firsthand just how important that mighty river was to the economy of the South, and unless it was completely controlled by the North, the Confederates would continue to bring in supplies, food, and soldiers. Additionally, total Union control of the Mississippi would split the Confederacy, leaving Texas, Arkansas, and Louisiana isolated. Vicksburg was the last piece of the puzzle in the West.

But this was no easy puzzle for Grant. For months, he and his army had been trying to dig, chop, and blast their way through the dense bayous north of Vicksburg. Grant felt that an approach by land rather than by river had the best chance of surprising the army in Vicksburg. But the land was so swampy that horses, carts, and even soldiers' feet got stuck. Grant had spent weeks directing the digging of a canal so that troops could float to Vicksburg, only to discover that the canal would not fill with water. Back in the East, people began to grumble and gossip again. Was Grant drunk? Was he just being lazy? Fire him!

As always, however, Lincoln continued to support his best leader.

"I think Grant has hardly a friend left, except myself!" Lincoln joked.

Finally Grant decided on a plan that even his closest general, William Tecumseh Sherman, thought was an exceptionally bad idea. Grant wanted to split the army. Sherman and half of the troops would march down along the Mississippi and fake an attack from the north. While this distracted and occupied the Confederate soldiers, Grant and his troops would continue marching south, cross the Mississippi well below Vicksburg, and attack the city from the south. No one would expect the Yankees to approach from the south.

It took Grant's army two weeks to march far enough south so that they could cross the Mississippi without the Confederates seeing them. On April 30, when Grant's army crossed the Mississippi River, Sherman and his troops attacked Vicksburg from the north. Instead of attacking Vicksburg from the south, Grant and his army marched northeast for another two weeks, arriving at Jackson, Mississippi's capital, which was forty miles east of Vicksburg. There they met up with Sherman's forces and launched an attack on Vicksburg from the east. The Confederates were so confused and surprised that they were running in all directions, and Union forces were able to surround the entire city. Grant's gamble, it seemed, had paid off. However, the 31,000 Confederate soldiers trapped within Vicksburg were not about to give up. Three times they were able to defend against the Yankees' attacks.

"Well, then," Grant calmly announced, "we'll lay siege to the place. We'll outcamp them."

By this, Grant meant that he intended to keep Vicksburg surrounded for as long as it took. No one would get out, and no people or supplies would get in.

"We were so tightly wrapped around Vicksburg," one Union soldier remembered, "that a cat could not have crept out without being discovered."

In time, Grant knew, both Confederate soldiers and civilians would grow desperate for food. Meanwhile, Grant ordered a constant firing of shells on the city in order to frighten the civilians and wear them down. Once residents' homes were tattered and blasted, they'd beg their soldiers to give up. Certainly, Grant felt, this siege would be over within a week.

But then an unusual thing happened. The people of Vicksburg, who had once been described as "not knowing how to surrender," literally dug caves into the surrounding hillsides for protection. Once caves were dug, residents hauled beds, cooking utensils, and even expensive tapestries into their new "homes" to wait out the siege. Stores of food were piled in separate cooler caves dug farther back.

"They'll never take this town!" one woman from Vicksburg proudly wrote in her diary. "We'll just burrow into these hills and let them batter away as hard as they please."

And so the Siege of Vicksburg dragged on for two weeks, three weeks, a month, and longer. Neither the civilians in their caves nor the opposing armies would budge one inch.

Back in Richmond, Jefferson Davis met with Robert E. Lee.

"Grant's a problem," he said with a frown. "We cannot afford to lose Vicksburg."

Lee knew what Davis wanted. If Lee would lead more soldiers to Vicksburg, it could possibly be saved. However, Lee had already come up with a plan that he thought was even better. Why not, Lee asked Davis, begin marching the Army of Northern Virginia north again? Lincoln would most likely panic and ask Grant to give up the siege in favor of rushing back to protect Washington. After all the bad luck Lincoln had had with his eastern generals, Grant was now the only general he could truly rely upon.

This seemed to Jefferson Davis like a reasonable plan, so in late May 1863, Lee led 70,000 men north once again. Many of these now-seasoned soldiers shared an anxious sense of urgency that they had not felt before. As they marched the same dusty roads they had traveled only ten months earlier, they knew that this time they *must* succeed in attacking the Yankees in their own territory.

"This army has never done such fighting as it will do now," a private from Virginia gravely predicted. "We will show the Yankees this time how we can fight."

Sooner than the young private knew, he would get his chance.

This time, as the Confederate army made its way into Maryland, it made no effort to win the people over with songs and friendliness. The soldiers were awfully ragged and beaten down. Many of them were starving, and all of them were anxious to get this horrible war over with. As the people of Maryland turned away in fright and disgust, the Rebels shouted rudely at them and, on occasion, shot their rifles into the air to scare them even more.

"And wasn't no freed slave free if we come across him," one Rebel recalled. Blacks who had come north after the Emancipation Proclamation dared not let the marching Confederates see them. Those who were unlucky enough to be spotted were often captured, tied up, and hauled back to the South.

Now as Lee and his shabby army moved into Pennsylvania, they sometimes took what they needed from farms, fields, stores, and even homes of civilians. By this point in the war, the South was suffering greatly—cities had been destroyed, rivers were blocked, acres and acres of farmland had been burned, and thousands of young men had been killed or crippled. Though the people who lived in the South refused to admit it, their homeland was slowly dying. Soon, nothing would be left. Therefore, a good part of Lee's motivation for heading north was to resupply and feed his troops. Always a man proud of his appearance, Lee could not bear to see his soldiers wearing rags and, worse yet, marching barefoot.

It was, then, on the morning of July 1, 1863, that part of Lee's army split off to go in search of shoes. There had been a rumor that there was a warehouse full of shoes in the small town of Gettysburg, Pennsylvania, and the Rebels were set on seizing the warehouse. On this very same day, a small Union cavalry force had decided, just by chance, to rest for a while in Gettysburg. Up until this moment, neither side had had a clue as to their enemy's whereabouts.

"We moved forward, leisurely smoking and chatting as we rode along," one Confederate later recalled. Then, as the Rebels approached Gettysburg, shots rang out. The startled Confederates immediately jumped into battle mode, firing back at the Union soldiers and shouting. When the Rebels realized they had more men than the smaller Yankee cavalry, they began pushing them back and then chasing them right through the main streets of Gettysburg.

"Hurry! Get out!" came the screams of the townspeople to one another. "We are about to be shelled!"

In a mass of confusion, the streets were filled with panicked residents running headlong into the clashing soldiers. Some people carried belongings and clothing. Some even had chickens and pigs tucked under their arms. Although the North had not experienced the same kind of destruction the South had, it was well known that Civil War battles left nothing behind but bodies and burning rubble. No one knew where to go, but everyone knew they could not stay in Gettysburg.

Through the town and up a hill, the Confederates continued pushing the Union troops back. Finally, the Yankees took cover and defensive positions along a ridge. Union general Winfield Scott Hancock ducked behind an arch and took a quick look around. Over his head, a swinging sign read: "ALL PERSONS FOUND USING FIREARMS IN THESE GROUNDS WILL BE PROSECUTED WITH THE UTMOST RIGOR OF THE LAW."

It was then that the general noticed the rows of low stones. By an odd twist of grim fate, the most terrible and deadly battle of the Civil War was about to begin—in a graveyard.

# CHAPTER 9

$\mathcal{A}$s night fell, the Union army settled into the area known as Cemetery Ridge. Facing them to the west, and nearly a mile away, the Confederate forces took up positions along another hillside named Seminary Ridge. When Robert E. Lee had heard about the sudden skirmish in Gettysburg, he was furious that his men had engaged in fighting without his permission. But now the skirmish had become a full-blown battle, and Lee rushed to the battle site. All night long, both Confederate and Union armies streamed into Gettysburg, preparing to resume the fight in the morning.

Before 4:00 a.m. on July 2, the pre-battle rumblings, drumbeats, and shouted commands began. Union general George Meade, who just four days earlier had replaced General Hooker as commander of the Army of the Potomac, was ready and confident. "I fully believe we shall whip these poor fellows," he announced. Still, Meade decided to let Lee make the first move, thereby allowing even more Union soldiers to reach Gettysburg. Although Lee's officers were usually well organized and quick to respond, things did not go smoothly on this day. As a result of poor communication and confusion, Lee's army did not begin the attack until nearly 4:00 in the afternoon. Having stalled so long, the Confederates now found themselves outnumbered by thousands of Union troops.

To the north and south of Cemetery Ridge were three hills named Big Round Top, Little Round Top, and Culp's Hill. Capturing these hills was critical; being able to place artillery on hilltops was a major advantage. Throughout the evening and into the night, the Confederates struggled to push the Yankees away from the hilltops. In areas known as Devil's Den, the Peach Orchard, and the Wheatfield, thousands of soldiers from both sides fell.

"The balls were whizzing so thick," one Rebel recalled, "that it looked like a man could hold out a hat and catch it full."

The Rebels pushed hard and were able to capture part of Culp's Hill. By day's end, however, the Union army had the upper hand. Because Meade had had so much time earlier in the day, he had been able to arrange his soldiers in better positions. To the Confederate soldiers, it seemed as though bullets were constantly raining on them from above. It was nearly impossible to make progress, and Lee and his men were in a difficult spot.

By the light of a full moon, Robert E. Lee and his top general, James Longstreet, discussed the battle plans for the next day. Lee decided to take a big risk and attack the Union forces head-on by charging across flat ground toward Cemetery Ridge. Lee bet that General Meade would send most of his men to the hilltops again. If the Confederates could charge quickly and strongly, they could take over the hills before Meade's men were in place. Longstreet could not have disagreed more with Lee's plan.

"This sort of unexpected charge across a field did not work so well for Burnside at Fredericksburg," Longstreet tersely reminded Lee. Late into the night, the two generals argued, but Lee insisted on his risky idea.

"Never was I so depressed as on that day," Longstreet recalled of the pre-battle morning of July 3, 1863. "I felt that my men were to be sacrificed, and that I should have to order them to make a hopeless charge."

At first, the morning's fighting focused on small repeated attacks on Culp's Hill in an attempt to fool Meade into believing that that was Lee's main focus. Quietly, however, thousands of Rebels got into position along Seminary Ridge for the principal attack. Early in the afternoon, 170 Confederate cannons erupted in unison, aiming their cannonballs at Cemetery Ridge in hopes of paving the way for the soldiers. It was the largest and loudest artillery bombardment of the entire war. People miles away from Gettysburg heard the cannon thunder, and some of the soldiers in charge of firing the cannons lost their hearing.

"Cemetery Hill and Ridge were ploughed and furrowed," a Union soldier remembered. "The flowers in bloom upon the graves at the Cemetery were shot away."

Union forces responded with a long and heavy barrage of their own. Then, around 2:30 in the afternoon, the Union cannons gradually fell silent, leading the Confederates to believe that the cannons had been destroyed. The time for the charge on Cemetery Ridge had arrived. The main division involved in the charge was under command of a young general named George Pickett. In the years to come, this infamous charge would be known as "Pickett's Charge." Now Pickett looked nervously to Longstreet, his commander, for the go-ahead.

"General, shall I advance?" Pickett finally asked. Longstreet was so distressed that he couldn't even bring himself to speak. Bowing his head, he simply raised his hand. The sign to advance had been given. Pickett's face went white with fear. For just a moment he prayed aloud, staring up at the smoky sky. Then an expression of pure determination replaced the fear.

"Up, men, and to your posts!" Pickett shouted boldly. "Don't forget today that you are from Old Virginia."

Thirteen thousand Confederate soldiers began marching quickly across the field in the steamy July afternoon. For once, however, they remained quiet. Their trademark Rebel yells and whooping were replaced by muffled marching through grass as a low drumbeat kept time. They moved with a solemn, almost sad, pride that impressed even the enemy.

"They came on in magnificent order," one Union soldier remembered with tears in his eyes, "with the step of men who believed themselves invincible. It was the most beautiful thing I ever saw."

However, in spite of the Yankees' admiration of the Rebels' courage, this was war. From their hilltop perches, the Union soldiers opened fire on the Rebels. The fields below filled with dense smoke and the moans of wounded and dying men. Still, row after row of determined Confederates moved onward toward Cemetery Ridge until the two armies were nearly face to face. Some of the most vicious fighting of the entire war took place that hot afternoon. Soldiers ran head-on into one another with gleaming bayonets. Rifles were fired at point-blank range, and men struggled in hand-to-hand combat using knives and even rocks. Sometimes the soldiers were so blinded by the smoke of gunfire that they didn't know if they were fighting the enemy or one of their own.

From the beginning, hilltop positions had given the Union army a clear advantage. In horror, General Pickett watched as half of his 13,000 men were either shot down or captured. Robert E. Lee had lost his gamble in a very big way. Now as Lee rode out among the soldiers, thousands began to turn and run in terror back to Seminary Ridge. Lee did not try to stop them. "It was all my fault!" he shouted again and again, nearly in tears. Although Lee would take the blame, some of his generals never forgave him for that battle. Years after Gettysburg, General Pickett scoffed at the name of Lee. "That old man had my division slaughtered," was all he would ever say about the Confederacy's greatest leader.

Gettysburg claimed more than 51,000 casualties. So many men had been killed that they lay in piles everywhere. Days after the battle, many bodies still had not been buried. It was a ghastly sight, as one Union soldier recalled:

"The dead bodies had lain there, putrefying under the summer sun for three days. Corpses were swollen to twice their original size. . . . Several human corpses sat upright against a fence, with arms extended in the air and faces hideous with something like a fixed leer, as if taking a fiendish pleasure in showing us what we essentially were and might at any moment be."

Barely twenty-four hours after the Union's victory at Gettysburg, General Grant and his soldiers finally broke the will of the people and the soldiers in Vicksburg, Mississippi. The siege had lasted longer than anyone had imagined it ever would. For forty-eight days, residents of Vicksburg had hidden in their caves.

"It was living like we were plant roots. And we were constantly in dread of snakes," one woman wrote after finding a rattlesnake curled up under her bed one morning.

Worse than dirt and snakes was the constant shelling by Union troops. The city of Vicksburg was in shambles, and every day more and more caves collapsed on top of their dwellers. Still, Vicksburg stubbornly refused to surrender. When food started running out, both soldiers and civilians began eating their horses, dogs, cats, and mules. Terrible, chewy bread made of dried peas and muddy water became a staple, and finally the people of Vicksburg were forced to eat rats. When the rats grew scarce, some cave dwellers boiled their own shoes and gnawed on the leather. However, some just went hungry.

"Fried rat tastes as good as squirrel, and I'll eat one any day," a young boy observed. "But I ain't eating my shoes."

Perhaps the Union soldiers' biggest problem during the siege was boredom. There was nothing to do but wait around the borders of the city, shelling it from time to time. It was widely reported that Grant got so blindingly drunk for a few days during this time that his generals had to move his camp so that his soldiers would not see him stumbling around. As for the soldiers, they typically entertained themselves with cards, gambling, writing letters, and playing music, but even this got dull after a few weeks. Some Yankees finally made friends with the Rebels just across the city's wide stone walls.

"On moonlit nights," a young Yankee recalled, "we used to agree to get up on the wall and just have a talk. Both sides would laugh and sing songs for an hour at a time, then get down and commence shooting again."

Finally, however, it was hunger that drove the Confederates to surrender. Rations got smaller and smaller, and finally the men were given nothing more than one biscuit a day. On July 2, a group of Rebels sent a letter to their commanding officer, John Pemberton, politely announcing that if he could not find a way to feed them, they would soon begin surrendering to the Yankees by themselves.

Pemberton had no choice. On July 4, 1863, the Confederate army surrendered.

At first, Grant intended to live up to his "unconditional surrender" nickname and take all 30,000 Rebel soldiers prisoner. On second thought, however, he decided to order these men to go home. Their starved and ragged condition would send a strong message to the people living in all the various areas of the South where these men were from: The North was winning. Thus, on the Fourth of July, the American flag was proudly raised over the Vicksburg courthouse, and the Confederate flag was taken down and burned.

When word of the victory reached Abraham Lincoln, he breathed a great sigh of relief. The Confederacy had been split in half. And, perhaps more important, the entire Mississippi River was now under the Union's guard and control.

"The Father of Waters," Lincoln famously said, "again goes unvexed to the sea."

It may have been a glorious Independence Day in Washington, but it definitely was not glorious in Vicksburg. Residents finally crawled out of their caves only to find their homes, businesses, and farms destroyed. Many people who lined the streets were in tears. When the citizens received the additional bitter news of the South's defeat at Gettysburg, some felt that it was the beginning of the end.

• • •

"This is no holiday for us," a furious Vicksburg woman wrote in her diary on July 4. "The murderous Yankees may celebrate it, but I will not. Never again!"

She was not alone in her anger. The Fourth of July would not be celebrated again in Vicksburg, Mississippi, until World War II.

The Confederate losses at both Vicksburg and Gettysburg marked the turning point of the Civil War. Although the South would win a few more defensive battles in the next year, the Confederates no longer had any hope of pushing into the North to force a victory. Now the Rebels were merely hanging on. The Confederate armies had dwindled to half their original size, and many of the soldiers still fighting were injured, sick, or starving. In addition, as the South began to crumble, the Union armies increased the intensity of their attacks in an effort to bring the awful war to an end.

Abraham Lincoln knew he had few, if any, fans in the South. He understood why he was hated in the Confederacy, but he was not happy about it. The toll the war was taking on the South disturbed Lincoln deeply.

"When I think of the sacrifices of life still to be offered, and the hearts and homes to be made lonely before this terrible war is over, my heart is like lead," Lincoln lamented. "I feel at times like hiding in a deep darkness."

In his heart, Lincoln believed that one day the South would be proud to be part of the United States and glad that their war of secession had not been successful. Keeping the Union whole was more important to Lincoln than anything else, and he sent the Union armies south not to punish Southerners but, rather, to keep them from making what he considered a terrible mistake.

Four months after the Battle of Gettysburg, the governor of Pennsylvania wrote to Abraham Lincoln. The summer and fall rains had washed away many of the shallow graves in the battlefield and, worse still, some soldiers had not even been properly buried yet. Coffins and bodies wrapped in blankets were scattered around the battleground. And the bones and carcasses of hundreds of horses lay where they had fallen. This was no way, the governor felt, to honor those who had given their lives to the cause of the Union.

Lincoln and the governor decided to turn the Gettysburg battlefield into a national cemetery for soldiers. Thus, on a cold, clear November morning, Lincoln spoke to the 9,000 people gathered on the Gettysburg battlefield for the dedication of the cemetery. A chilly wind whistled through the Peach Orchard and around the hilltops where so many men had fallen. Lincoln looked out across the somber crowd, and then he began to speak in his high, clear, emotional voice:

"Fourscore and seven years ago our fathers brought forth on this continent a new nation, conceived in liberty and dedicated to the proposition that all men are created equal . . ."

Only 267 words long, Lincoln's Gettysburg Address may have been one of the shortest speeches the President ever gave, yet it touched people deeply. Lincoln's main message was that the soldiers had given their lives so that "that nation might live." The dedication of the field to the soldiers' memory, Lincoln said, was nothing compared to the dedication the young soldiers had shown to their country.

"We here highly resolve that these dead shall not have died in vain," Lincoln concluded, "that this nation, under God, shall have a new birth of freedom, and that government of the people, by the people, for the people shall not perish from the earth."

# CHAPTER 10

"*W*e are starving! As soon as enough of us get together, we are going to the bakeries and each of us will take a loaf of bread. That is little enough for the government to give us after it has taken all our men!"

These were the angry shouts of women in Richmond, Virginia, in 1863. Everyone in the South was weary of the war, but women, who had been left behind to deal with farms, children, and the terror of invading Yankees, had reached a breaking point. Making matters worse, by 1863 money was almost worthless in the South. The Confederacy had decided to print its own money, and when the South began losing the war, the value of Confederate dollars dropped quickly. This decreased value, in turn, created inflation. In some parts of the South, a loaf of bread could cost as much as fifty Confederate dollars! These high prices, then, are what sparked the Southern Bread Riots.

In cities throughout the South, angry mobs made up mostly of women stormed into stores and grabbed food, clothing, and even jewelry. In Richmond, the women became so rowdy that President Jefferson Davis tried to calm them down with a speech. When that didn't work, he threw them money from his own pockets.

"Look! This is all I have!" he shouted desperately as he tossed worthless coins and bills at the women who were closing in on him and shaking their fists. "I have no more money!"

When this failed, Davis called in the militia and ordered them to fire at the women if they did not return to their homes. Reluctantly and with plenty of grumbling, the women finally gave up their protest.

The helplessness that women in the South were experiencing added to their fear and anger. Many thousands of women went for months and even years without knowing whether their husbands, fathers, brothers, or sons were dead or alive. Many women fought this helpless feeling by taking over the jobs that the men were forced to leave behind. But some women fought the helplessness in a more unusual way: They actually joined the military effort.

More than a few young women took up arms and marched into battles disguised as men, with their hats pulled low and their uniforms baggy enough to discourage suspicion. It's hard to know exactly how many women secretly became soldiers, but it's believed that at least several hundred made their way into battle. One Cuban-born woman living in the South, Loreta Janeta Velazquez, was so determined to stay near her enlisted husband that she pasted a beard and moustache on her face and passed herself off as Lieutenant Harry T. Buford. In four days, she recruited 236 men, which she sent to her husband, who was commanding a unit in Florida. Velazquez claimed to have participated in several battles, including Bull Run and Shiloh, before she was shot in the side and her female identity became known.

Women who were discovered pretending to be male soldiers were, of course, sent home with a stern warning not to interfere with the war ever again. However, as the war progressed, both the North and the South found an unusual way women could "fight" for their side. In the 1800s, no one expected a young woman to be capable of doing much more than raising children, tending to a husband, and keeping a house in order. This, then, was exactly what made women perfect for working as spies.

One of the most famous spies of the Civil War was Rose O'Neal Greenhow, who was better known as "Wild Rose" and "Rebel Rose." Rose lived in

Washington, D.C., but she sympathized with the South. By all accounts, she was a brilliant and beautiful woman. Men—even Yankee officers— could not resist her charms. Although most Union officers and politicians knew that Rose supported the South, this didn't keep them from attending the many parties and dinners she hosted in her Washington home. There, the conversations flowed along with the wine, and Rose was not shy about using her flirtatious nature to get the information she wanted.

"I employed every capacity with which God has endowed me," Rose later said of her attempts to coax secret information out of the Union men who came to her dinners. "The result was far more successful than my hopes could have flattered me to expect."

Rose obtained so much information that Jefferson Davis credited her for the Confederacy's victory at the First Battle of Bull Run. Only days before the battle, Rose had sent a secret ten-word message to one of the Confederate generals, letting him know when and where the Union army was going to attack. Perhaps the Union officers who had been so startled and surprised by the Rebels' counterattack at Bull Run had been the very ones who had gotten just a little too friendly with Wild Rose at one of her famous parties.

• • •

While women in the South protested the war by raiding bakeries, some men in the North protested by participating in draft riots. The North now had the momentum, but there was still a lot of war left to fight. Gettysburg had been an important victory for the Union, but the stunning death toll scared people. Young men who had once rushed to sign up to fight for the Union now stayed away. At the same time, 300,000 more troops were needed for the Union army. Finally, Abraham Lincoln had no other choice—he issued a draft call. Throughout the North, many men were very angry about the possibility of being drafted, or called into required military service. Adding to their anger was a newly passed bill that allowed those who could pay a fee of three hundred dollars to be excused from serving.

"This is a rich man's bill!" one congressman complained. "The sons of rich men will be spared, while the sons of the working man will be sent off to their death."

In 1863, three hundred dollars was a lot of money. Although few families had that kind of money, those who did were suddenly able to buy their husband's or son's way out of the danger of the battlefield. Many people were furious that the government would allow such an obvious injustice.

Perhaps no group of people was more upset about the draft than new immigrants from Ireland. Many of these Irish people were very poor, and they could ill afford to lose the heads of their sometimes very large families. Further fueling their anger, many Irish people had no interest in fighting a war that now focused on the freedom of blacks, a race of people they knew nothing about. And making matters worse, newly freed blacks were now competing with the Irish for many of the Northern cities' lowest-paying jobs. This often created bad feelings between the Irish and the blacks.

In New York City in July, an angry mob made up mostly of Irish men stormed the draft office and destroyed it. Then they took off running down the streets, setting fire to buildings and targeting black people as the victims of their frustration. Soon, more and more people joined in. Many of these people were not so much opposed to the draft as they were just sick and tired of the war and looking for a way to blow off steam.

One woman described the mob as "thousands of infuriated creatures, yelling, screaming, and swearing." She continued, "The rush and roar grew every moment more terrific . . . men with red, swollen faces, brandishing sticks and clubs, and boys, women, and children hurrying on and joining with them in this mad chase up the avenue like a company of raging fiends."

The rioting went on for four days. More than one black man was chased down, hanged, and set on fire. An orphanage for black children was burned to the ground. Loud voices booed Abraham Lincoln and cheered Jefferson Davis. In the end, at least 120 people were killed and thousands were injured.

But as tired of the war as many Northerners had become, most of the Union soldiers and their generals remained determined. The direction of the war had changed quite dramatically for the North, and now the Civil War must end victoriously for the Union, regardless of how long it took.

*"We must succeed!"* wrote one soldier. "If not this year, why then the next, or the next. And if it takes ten years, then ten years it must be, for we never can give up."

And so the draft, like the war, would continue.

As 1863 rolled on, Union forces in the West, led by Ulysses S. Grant, began pushing eastward now that the Mississippi River was in Union control. Grant was still the only general that Lincoln had complete faith in, and Lincoln wanted to place Grant in charge of *all* the armies in the West as soon as possible. Unfortunately, this didn't happen soon enough.

In mid-September, Union and Confederate forces clashed in a small skirmish in Chickamauga, a small town in the northwest corner of Georgia. Like the many thousands of skirmishes during the Civil War, this began as a random exchange of fire between two small groups. But gradually, more troops joined in, and eventually this turned into a full-blown battle.

In charge of the Union forces was General William Rosencrans, an indecisive and nervous man whom Lincoln once described as behaving "like a duck hit on the head." As the fighting along Chickamauga Creek grew fiercer, Rosencrans faltered and made a terrible error: He sent soldiers to close a gap that didn't even exist. As a result, a *real* gap, nearly a quarter mile long, opened up along the Union line.

Suddenly, the Rebels were pouring through the gap and surrounding the Yankees. Troops from both sides were so entwined and fighting so closely that the casualties, as in Gettysburg, were astounding. More than 4,000 men were killed in two days of fighting, and the Union forces were pushed back to nearby Chattanooga, Tennessee. As luck would have it, Rosencrans had actually been successful at driving Confederate troops out of Chattanooga only a week earlier. Now, embarrassingly, the Confederates had not only returned to Chattanooga, they had trapped the Union army inside a corner of the city.

"Starvation is the surest weapon," a Confederate soldier wrote as the South waited out a siege on the cornered Yankees. As Grant had done in Vicksburg, the Confederates now hoped to starve troops into surrender. For weeks, no supplies got past the Rebel guards, and Yankee soldiers resorted to dining on mice, garbage, and even tree bark while General Rosencrans fretted and did nothing.

Lincoln had had enough. He now put U.S. Grant in charge of all Union armies between the Appalachian Mountains and the Mississippi. The War in the West would be won once the Union armies had control of Tennessee. Then, because of all the railroads that passed through Chattanooga, the path to invading the Deep South would be wide open. Decisive action and strong leadership had never been more important, and Lincoln was in no mood to see the march through Tennessee stalled by a jittery General Rosencrans. On Lincoln's orders, Grant rushed to Chattanooga and immediately went to work.

"We began to see things move," one Union soldier said of Grant's arrival. "We felt that everything came from a plan."

And the plan worked. Grant quickly found a hole in the Confederate trap and sent in all the supplies needed. Not only was Grant determined to break the Union army out of the trap that the Rebels had caught them in, he wanted to drive away the Confederates altogether and claim victory over Chattanooga. It seemed like an impossible plan at first. The Rebel forces had set up camps on two hilltops: Missionary Ridge and Lookout Mountain. Aside from their superior position, the Confederates also had more men—but not for long.

Up from Mississippi came General Sherman with 20,000 soldiers. And down from Virginia rushed

General Hooker with another 15,000 men. Quick plans were put together, and the Yankees suddenly attacked their captors. The loss at Chickamauga had been particularly bitter for Union soldiers, and now they shouted, "Chickamauga! Chickamauga!" as they charged the Chattanooga hillsides for three days. The fog was so dense on Lookout Mountain, that the battle there would forever be remembered as "the Battle Above the Clouds." No one would have believed that the Union could have won back Chattanooga, but seventy-two hours later, they had.

As 1863 drew to a close, the stunned Confederates quickly retreated south to Georgia. This was exactly what General Grant wanted. He had another plan ready, and this time it involved sending his favorite general, William Tecumseh Sherman, on a merciless rampage through the Deep South, starting with Georgia. Sherman had had his ups and downs during the Civil War, once even being accused of insanity after demanding an army of 200,000 men for a single battle in Kentucky. Still, Grant had never lost faith in his friend.

"Grant stood by me when I was crazy, and I stood by him when he was drunk," Sherman said wryly before heading to Georgia, "and now we stand by each other."

Sherman had a reputation as a ferocious and heartless man who seemed to take joy in the gruesome battles he fought. In reality, like most great generals, Sherman despised war. "I am tired and sick of war. Its glory is all moonshine," Sherman said in 1864. "It is only those who have neither fired a shot nor heard the shrieks and groans of the wounded who cry aloud for blood, for vengeance, for desolation. War is hell."

Nonetheless, Sherman was determined to move quickly and brutally through Georgia and beyond. He wanted the war to end, and he knew that it would not end until the South and her people were utterly broken. Thus, as he headed out in the spring of 1864, General Sherman announced that he did not care if the people of the South hated him forever; he was going to do what had to be done.

"War is war, and not popularity seeking," Sherman said grimly. "I intend to make Georgia howl."

Meanwhile, as a result of his remarkable victory at Chattanooga, Grant was to receive yet another promotion from President Lincoln. The evening before he was appointed to lieutenant general, in command of *all* the Union forces in the United States, Grant was summoned to the White House by President Lincoln. A shy man of few words, Grant was nervous about meeting the President for the first time. But Lincoln, even though he towered over Grant by nearly a foot, put the general at ease with a broad smile, a joke, and a warm handshake.

Grant's ease, however, was short-lived. As Lincoln and his guest entered the brightly lit East Room of the White House, Grant was mortified to see that a large reception was going on—and *he* was the person that everyone wanted to meet. The cheering and curious crowd gathered closely around him, shaking his hand and slapping him on the back. When those in the back of the crowd shouted that they could not see the famous general, Grant was asked to step up onto a sofa so that everyone could get a better look at him. It was, for the modest and often bashful Grant, a nightmare come true.

"He blushed like a schoolgirl," one reporter wrote. "The little scared-looking man who stood on a crimson-covered sofa was the idol of the hour."

Tongue-tied and sweating, Grant endured nearly two hours of reporters asking questions, young women flirting, and important politicians trying to impress him. Grant later indicated that leading a battle was nothing compared to the torture of that reception. As soon as he could graciously do so, Grant left—and he returned to the White House on another day to discuss the business of war with the President. The two men had great confidence in one another, Lincoln not needing to know Grant's plan but Grant choosing to share it anyway.

"All I want or have ever wanted is someone who will take responsibility and act," Lincoln explained to Grant.

Grant made sure that all of his generals knew the plan as well. The strategy was to have the various Union armies attack the Confederates at one time, thereby making it impossible for the Confederate armies to reinforce one another. As in the case of Chickamauga, a skirmish became a battle only when thousands of troops were sent in from both sides. Now, Grant was going to do his best to keep the South from being able to match the North's reinforcements.

Grant knew what this meant. It was time for what Lincoln hoped would be the final push to capture Richmond. Every attempt by the Union's Army of the Potomac to overtake the Confederate capital had failed. No one could seem to outsmart or overpower the wily General Robert E. Lee and his Army of Northern Virginia. But now the Union's toughest, wisest, and most successful general was going to go after Richmond.

For some time, people from Maine to Texas had been anticipating this turn of events, either with excitement or with dread. As one woman in Virginia put it, "It was bound to happen. We all knew it— we just didn't know when." But now the moment had arrived. It was time for the Civil War's ultimate showdown: Grant versus Lee.

## CHAPTER 11

"*I* am heartily tired of hearing what Lee is going to do," General Grant barked at his generals. "Some of you seem to think he is suddenly going to turn a double somersault and land on both our flanks at the same time. Go back to your command, and try to think of what we are going to do ourselves."

The Army of the Potomac had never seen a leader like Grant, and some of the soldiers were not sure, at first, whether they liked this new style of leadership. After a string of generals who had often been lazy, slow, timid, or dull-witted, it was a bit of a shock to suddenly have a general who was none of the above. As for Grant, he was not used to officers and soldiers who constantly worried and fretted about what the opposing side might do. It made Grant angry.

"But, sir," one of Grant's generals replied, "with all due respect, you have never tangled with a general like Bobby Lee before."

Grant did not argue with that point. Grant had heard plenty about Robert E. Lee, and he knew Lee was a tremendous leader who was not to be taken lightly. Still, Grant was confident that there was no way the Union could be beaten by Lee's army this time around. It was now simply a matter of numbers—the North had nearly three times as many soldiers as the South. And of the South's soldiers, a great many were too sick or too injured to be of much use.

To make things even more difficult for the Rebels, the prisoner exchange policy had been stopped. The policy had allowed soldiers who had been taken prisoner during battle to be returned to their homes if they were injured. Once these men were nursed back to health, they often returned to fighting, particularly in the South where soldiers were in short supply. Treatment of black prisoners by the Confederate army—and the increase in the number of black soldiers after the Emancipation Proclamation of 1863—had led to the abandonment of the prisoner exchange policy. Many people, in both the North and the South, were very upset about this decision. Forcing wounded men to die in prison seemed inhumane. Grant supported this new way of handling prisoners, however. Like Sherman, he was willing to do whatever had to be done to end the war—regardless of lives lost, and regardless of what people thought of him.

It was with this mindset that Grant led the Army of the Potomac toward Richmond. The spring of 1864 marked the beginning of what was known as "total war," a year-long period of continuous and all-out battle against the Confederacy. Lincoln and Grant had been in agreement: The South would not surrender until it ran out of soldiers and resources. Total destruction of land, businesses, farms, and even homes, then, was the goal during the final year of the Civil War.

Grant's and Lee's armies would first clash at the Wilderness, the same wooded area near Chancellorsville, Virginia, where the two armies had fought one another a year earlier. Bones and entire skeletons of both horses and humans littered the tangled woods. Disgusted and a bit frightened, Grant ordered some of his men to quickly bury the remains as the troops got into position. The fighting there would go on for three days and claim nearly 30,000 casualties. Grant had never fought in such heavy woods, and though his army outnumbered Lee's, Lee outmaneuvered Grant. Lee knew the woods well, and he knew how to fight in them. Finally, Grant ordered his men to fall back.

At first, the Confederates celebrated. They had beaten the Yankees in Virginia *again*, and this time they had won against the North's most famous general! The Army of Northern Virginia turned south to head back toward Richmond. The Rebels assumed that, as always, the Yankees would retreat to Washington and spend a month or more recovering before they attacked again. But then something happened that had never happened before.

"If you see the President, tell him from me that whatever happens, there will be no turning back," Grant had said to a news reporter at the Battle of the Wilderness. For the first time ever, the Army of the Potomac would pursue Lee's army instead of retreating. This meant no rest, no recovery, and barely time for the Yankees to catch their breath. But suddenly they didn't care.

"Our spirits rose," one Yankee soldier recalled. "Instead of heading north, we were headed south! Suddenly, the men all began to sing."

The singing, however, did not last long. The next battle, in the nearby town of Spotsylvania, would begin the very next day and last for nearly two weeks. The Union forces now outnumbered the Confederates 100,000 to 52,000, but once again, Lee knew the area better and had a superior battle strategy. The fighting was brutal, close, and relentless. Many of the soldiers became so frustrated and angry that they climbed the defense walls each side had built and shot straight down at their opponents. Still, neither side would retreat one inch from the line that separated the two armies.

"I intend to fight it out on this line if it takes all summer," Grant announced stubbornly.

If Lee's tactics relied on positioning and strategy, Grant's relied on the sheer number of soldiers he had. If one thousand of his men were killed, one thousand more were immediately sent in. And so it went until both sides were too exhausted to continue. Once again, there was no clear winner. Even Grant, in all his stubbornness, finally had to admit it: "Continuing this battle," he reluctantly said, "would be like knocking our heads against a brick wall." Finally, both sides retreated. Nearly twice as many Union soldiers had been killed as Confederates, but Grant would not slow down. He knew that if his army was exhausted, Lee's army must be even more exhausted. And so the Army of the Potomac continued to follow Lee south.

Now the opposing armies found themselves in something of a race: Whichever side reached the next battle site first would have a huge advantage. The ability to dig in, hide, and watch the enemy approach was, in many ways, more important than the number of soldiers an army had. Robert E. Lee was the first to arrive in the small crossroads of Cold Harbor. Grant knew how terribly dangerous it was to send his men straight into the waiting and hidden Confederate forces. All of the previous Union generals would have turned around and gone home, but Grant refused to give up.

"I'd seen a lot of battles," one Rebel general

recalled, "but never had I seen bloodshed like this. It wasn't war; it was murder."

Nearly 7,000 Union soldiers had been either killed or wounded, most within the first eight minutes of the battle. Because of their superior positions, far fewer Confederates had fallen. So many Union soldiers were killed that their bodies, piled several deep, covered more than five acres of ground. Finally, Grant ordered his men to fall back while he figured out what to do. Perhaps, he suggested to his generals, another attack should be made quickly to confuse the Rebels.

"I will not take my regiment in another such charge if Jesus Christ himself should order it!" one furious general shouted.

All of Grant's generals agreed—this had been a foolish and wasteful attack. Eventually, even Grant backed down, admitting that he had made a mistake. For three days, both the Yankees and Rebels did nothing except wait anxiously for the other side to make a move. Even collecting the wounded on the battlefield would be admitting defeat, so Grant waited, refusing to send men out to help the injured. Some wounded men became so desperate with pain that they shot themselves. One man was seen slitting his own throat with his bayonet.

"Grant is a butcher!" Mary Lincoln complained to her husband. "He has no regard for life . . . I could fight an army as well myself!"

The famous general who had so recently been swarmed by admiring crowds was once again criticized and labeled a murderer. In one month alone, Grant's army had suffered about 50,000 casualties. This was nearly one-third the number of Union casualties in the first two *years* of the war. Many Americans agreed with the First Lady: Grant was a madman, and he needed to be kicked out of command. But Abraham Lincoln would not interfere, trusting that Grant would eventually lead the Union to victory. And so Grant kept pressing toward Richmond. In the middle of a moonless night, he sneaked his army out of Cold Harbor and continued south.

When Lee realized what Grant had done, he ordered a hurried march to Richmond, believing that the Yankees were headed toward the Confederate capital. This, however, was one of the few times during the Civil War that Robert E. Lee was fooled. Instead of going to Richmond, Grant surrounded the town of Petersburg, Virginia, twenty miles south of Richmond. Petersburg was a major railroad center, and nearly all supplies for Richmond passed through it. Grant knew that if the Union army could capture Petersburg, Richmond would be crippled.

Barely 3,000 Rebel soldiers protected Petersburg when Grant's generals arrived with 16,000 men. It looked as though it would be a swift victory. Even Lincoln was optimistic and sent

Grant a brief message: "I begin to see it. You will succeed." However, success would come slowly. The Confederates had strong fortifications built around the city, and it was nearly impossible for Union soldiers to get past them. Fearing another Cold Harbor type of slaughter, Grant ordered his men to fall back and build their own fortifications.

Soon another siege was under way. The two sides would spend nearly ten months shooting back and forth at one another in a series of battles. In the North, many people saw this siege as pointless. Why not just attack Richmond and get it over with? But Grant knew what he was doing. Robert E. Lee kept sending more soldiers from Richmond in an attempt to drive Grant's army away, but this proved to be unsuccessful and costly. All Lee managed to do was lose more men. The summer of 1864 turned to fall and then to winter, and Lee's army continued to dwindle. The long-awaited news spread excitedly throughout the North: The Confederate Army of Northern Virginia was dying. The fall of Richmond was now only a matter of time.

And, just like that, Grant was suddenly a hero again.

On September 3, 1864, General Sherman sent a telegram to the government in Washington, D.C.: "Atlanta is ours, and fairly won." For months, the Confederates guarding Atlanta had tried to avoid battle with Sherman's much bigger army, but finally President Davis ordered the Southern forces to attack the invader. After weeks of lopsided fighting, the desperate Confederate army managed to escape just before Sherman's men had completely surrounded the city. Atlanta was now in Union control, but that was not enough to satisfy Sherman.

"War is cruelty," Sherman explained. "We are not only fighting hostile armies, but a hostile people, and we must make old and young, rich and poor, feel the hard hand of war."

Sherman felt that Atlanta, along with Richmond, had been the powerhouse behind the Confederacy. The Civil War had continued as long as it had because of the ongoing support from Atlanta, and now Sherman wanted the city destroyed. He ordered Atlanta to be hastily evacuated, and then he had his soldiers set fire to it. The infamous "Burning of Atlanta" destroyed much of the city, though some historians argue that it was not as dramatic or terrible as history has made it out to be. Those who lived in Atlanta in 1864 would probably disagree.

"Hell has laid her egg," one Atlantan wrote as he watched his city burn from a nearby hillside, "and right here it hatched."

Sherman and his army paused to gaze at the smoldering city on the morning of November 15, 1864. If Sherman felt any regret, he never expressed it. On the contrary, he routinely defended his actions by pointing out that the sooner the spirit of the South was broken, the sooner the terrible war would end. And the sooner the war ended, the sooner young men—from both sides—would cease to be slaughtered. With this in mind, Sherman turned his massive army of 64,000 men to the south and embarked on a long trek of utter destruction from Atlanta to Savannah, Georgia, in what would come to be known as "Sherman's March to the Sea."

Up to this point in the war, both sides had generally followed an unwritten rule when marching through enemy territory. Perhaps soldiers stole food and supplies from civilians now and then, but stealing or destroying the property of innocent people was frowned upon. This all changed with Sherman's March.

Sherman's men looted the slaves' cabins as well as the rich plantations. Yards were torn up in an effort to find jewelry and money that might have been buried by fleeing Georgians. So thorough was the search for anything of value that one slave watched soldiers dig up and examine a dead dog he had just buried. After taking what they wanted, Sherman's men trampled the fields and shot all the livestock to ensure that the people of Georgia would have nothing to eat. Even horses were slaughtered so that nothing of any value remained. Finally, the Union soldiers set fire to the homes and farms and businesses, and continued marching, often singing loudly as they went.

"For miles, the flames shot into the night sky," one woman wrote in her diary. "We watched the fires and heard the songs grow closer, knowing we would be next. We hated it so! But then there was nothing to do but take the children and what we could carry—and run, in fear and desperation, into the night."

By late December, Sherman and his army had left a path of devastation 60 miles wide and nearly 300 miles long. When the Yankees finally reached Savannah, the Rebels had only 10,000 soldiers in place to defend that important port city. Nonetheless, the Confederates had dug into hidden and well-protected defensive positions. Rather than engage in what would certainly be a long and bloody battle, Sherman simply explained in a letter to the Confederate generals that they had no chance of winning. And he casually mentioned that he had obtained special weapons from the Union navy: "I have already received guns that can cast heavy and destructive shot as far as the heart of your city."

Three days later, the Confederate army quietly escaped from Savannah, and Union soldiers entered the city.

On December 22, 1864, Sherman sent a telegram to President Lincoln: "I beg to present you as a Christmas gift the City of Savannah."

It may have been a "gift" from one of Lincoln's top generals, but the South had paid for it. Sherman himself estimated that his march had caused more than 100 million dollars of destruction. Some areas that had been poor to begin with would take nearly a century to fully recover. Years later, a war historian would accurately describe what Sherman had accomplished: "Sherman's raid succeeded in 'knocking the Confederate war effort to pieces.'"

Many of Sherman's soldiers whooped and hollered and wanted to celebrate the success of the march, but Sherman ordered them to be quiet, even threatening to physically punish those who did not obey.

"He took no joy in the misfortunes of others," one soldier recalled of Sherman. "He did what had to be done, but it was a grim business for him."

And the grim business would continue. In January of 1865, Sherman headed north, destroying the cities of Charleston and Columbia, South Carolina. This time the destructive path was nearly forty miles wide. So much was burned that many referred to Sherman's course as "the Black Path." Sherman punished South Carolina especially severely since it had been the first state to secede from the Union. Then he continued into North Carolina, and finally, his march came to an end as his troops approached Virginia. There Sherman planned to meet up with Grant, combining their massive armies and, at long last, bringing the terrible war to a close.

Throughout the North, people smelled victory. The roads to Grant's and Sherman's successes had not always been pretty, but now the Union was clearly winning. Abraham Lincoln, who only a year earlier had been strongly criticized for the way he was handling the war, now won reelection, soundly defeating his opponent—former general, George McClellan. Lincoln was relieved to have won. He had worried that another President might not work as hard as he planned to work to help rebuild the ravaged South when the war ended. He was deeply concerned that Southerners know that he did not intend to punish them.

"With malice toward none; with charity for all," Lincoln famously said in his second inaugural address, ". . . let us bind up the nation's wounds."

Nonetheless, Lincoln was thankful that his two best generals had finally gotten a strong grip on the fierce and determined Confederates. Comparing Grant and Sherman to two great hunters that work together to bring down a beast, Lincoln said, "Grant has the bear by the hind leg, while Sherman takes off its hide."

## CHAPTER 12

"*We* must choose whether the Negroes shall fight for us, or against us," a frustrated Robert E. Lee said to the Confederate Congress in Richmond. The Confederate forces had grown so thin that large gaps had opened up around both the besieged Petersburg and, now, Richmond. Thousands of slaves were still in the South, and now Lee was proposing that they be armed to fight for the Confederate cause.

The roomful of men stirred uneasily. Give guns to slaves? Wouldn't that be dangerous?

"If slaves will make good soldiers," a representative from Georgia said quietly, "our whole theory of slavery is wrong."

A silence fell over the room. Finally it had come to this. The South was so desperate for soldiers that it was willing to enlist the very men it aimed to keep enslaved. There was a time when President Davis had mocked Lincoln's decision to enlist black men, calling it the most disgusting decision "recorded in the history of guilty man." Now Davis hung his head and gave approval.

On March 20, 1865, residents of Richmond looked out their windows to see a strange sight: Rows of black soldiers marched in practice drills down Main Street as a band played "Dixie." Perhaps more than strange, the sight was chilling. This was undoubtedly a sign that the Confederacy was on its last legs. The slaves had been promised neither freedom nor money if they fought, but many felt they had no choice. As always, they felt obligated to do what a white man told them to do. As it would turn out, however, the war would be over before any of these forcibly enlisted black men would have to fight.

Reinforcements continued to swell the ranks of Grant's army in Petersburg, as they had all winter. The Rebel forces, on the other hand, had been reduced so that they were about a third the size of the Yankees' forces. Many of the Confederate soldiers were dying of starvation. Thousands of deserters, fed up with fighting a war they couldn't win, had simply walked away from the frontlines. The line of soldiers around the city should have been a thick crowd of men, but now it was reduced to single soldiers spaced twenty feet apart.

"It was not a line," one writer recounted. "It was the mere skeleton of a line."

By the end of March, Lee faced the hard truth: Grant's army was simply too powerful. Petersburg could no longer resist, and it finally fell to the Union's repeated attacks.

Despite the surrender, Robert E. Lee was no less determined.

He was "like a brave old lion brought to bay at last," one of Lee's colonels wrote, "determined to resist to the death, and if die it must, to die game."

Lee saw that he had one final chance. He could gather what was left of his army of Northern Virginia in Richmond, and they could all escape farther south to North Carolina. Waiting there was another army that had hidden in the hills during Sherman's raid. Perhaps, Lee thought desperately, the combined armies could rebuild and strengthen. *Perhaps* there was still a sliver of a chance that the Confederacy would not die.

However, this time Grant was a step ahead of Lee.

"I was afraid, every morning, that I would awake from my sleep to hear that Lee had gone," Grant would later write. "I knew he could move more rapidly than I, and that, if he got the start, he would leave me behind."

Grant knew that if Lee escaped, the war would continue to drag on. Even if the Yankees captured Richmond, the war would not end until Lee himself was cornered and forced to give up. Therefore,

Grant sent armies of Union soldiers to every escape route he could think of. Grant and Sherman pored over maps, tracing roads and trails and rivers and creeks. By the morning of April 2, 1865, Union soldiers stood guard at all points south and west of Richmond, waiting to meet Lee.

"Richmond must be evacuated this evening," Lee wrote in a hasty message to Confederate President Jefferson Davis. Davis was in a church service when he received the note, and those sitting around him saw his face turn slightly gray with shock. But Lee was planning his escape and taking his army with him. Without an army to guard it, Richmond would most certainly be under Union control within hours. That afternoon, Confederate troops set fire to food warehouses and grain mills in Richmond so that there would be nothing left for Union soldiers. Then they destroyed bridges leading into Richmond in an effort to slow the Yankees' descent upon the city that had been the Confederate capital for three years. Amid the smoke and soldiers, ran mobs of shouting people looking to loot stores, homes, and even saloons. After all, if the Yankees were going to take over Richmond, why should *anything* be left behind for them? One eyewitness watched great kegs of whiskey being thrown into the streets from a second-story warehouse window.

"Whiskey ran in the gutters ankle deep," he remembered. "Half-drunken women, and children even, fought to dip up the coveted fluid in tin pans, buckets, or any vessel available."

Finally, Richmond was evacuated very late that night. Confederate soldiers brought up the rear, throwing explosives on the last of the Confederate fleet anchored in the nearby James River. Like a fireworks display bidding the Rebels farewell, the ammunition stored in the ships noisily blew up and shot streaks of fire high into the air. Some soldiers recalled seeing the fiery display from more than three miles outside of Richmond.

Remaining behind in Richmond, however, were thousands of residents who eagerly awaited the Union troops' arrival. Very early on the morning of April 3, a rumbling cheer from these people grew louder and louder as the Yankees began streaming in.

"From the colored population of Richmond we received such a reception as could only come from a people who were returning thanks for deliverance of their race," one soldier commented.

As the Stars and Stripes replaced the Confederate flag over the capitol, former slaves sang, shouted, and hugged one another. Many of them ran up to soldiers and threw their arms around them, weeping with joy. The few white people who had remained in Richmond for various reasons were appalled by the behavior of their former slaves and servants. A black Union soldier had been sent to guard Robert

E. Lee's wife who had been too ill to travel. When Mrs. Lee looked out her window and saw that a black man was protecting her, she grew angry and confused.

"This is, perhaps, an insult," she announced uncertainly to a commanding Union officer. When a white Union soldier took the black soldier's place, Mrs. Lee politely sent him breakfast on a silver tray.

The next day, President Lincoln arrived in Richmond. At six feet five inches tall and wearing his trademark stovepipe hat, the tall thin man towered over most of the crowd that surrounded him. However, Lincoln did not look like the same man who had become President just four years earlier. His wavy, unruly black hair was streaked with gray, and his face was wrinkled with deep lines of worry. Although he smiled as he greeted the crowd that morning, a sorrow in his eyes revealed the four years of heartbreak and agony.

"Thank God I have lived to see this," Lincoln said with a sad smile as he gazed up at the Stars and Stripes above the Confederate capitol. "It seems to me that I have been dreaming a horrid nightmare for four years, and now the nightmare is over."

In a respectful, almost formal manner, many black people approached Lincoln just to shake his hand, touch his coat sleeve, thank him, or even kneel before him. A reporter who was covering the events noted that one elderly black man walked up to Lincoln, took off his hat, bowed, and with tears streaming down his face said, "May the good Lord bless you."

"The President removed his own hat," the reporter wrote, "and bowed in silence. But it was a bow which upset the forms, laws, customs, and ceremonies of centuries [of slavery]."

Then Lincoln stepped inside the quiet Confederate capitol and walked to President Jefferson Davis's own desk. Lincoln sat down behind the desk, folded his hands, and absorbed the significance of the occasion. It was a symbolic moment. The capital of the Confederate government had fallen, and Lincoln was once again president of a united country.

Now, there was one last piece of the war puzzle that remained before the Civil War could be brought to a close: Robert E. Lee and his army must be stopped.

Lee and the ragged remnants of his army had marched nonstop as they headed southwest toward North Carolina. Many of the soldiers had had no food in days, and now they gnawed on handfuls of dried corn meant for the horses. Lee rode swiftly back and forth along the line of men, encouraging them and trying to keep their spirits up. But Lee knew what lay ahead, and even as he assured his men that they would escape the Yankees, 120,000 Union soldiers were closing in on Lee's 25,000 soldiers from all directions.

Finally, on April 7, the Confederates were surrounded near the Appomattox River. Grant sent Lee a message politely pointing out the hopelessness of Lee's position and suggesting that in order to prevent further bloodshed he consider surrendering the Army of Northern Virginia. Although some of his own officers believed that the time for surrender had come, Lee refused.

"What will my country think of me if I do not continue to fight?" he angrily asked one of his officers.

"Country be damned!" the officer responded. "There *is* no country. There has been no country for a year or more!"

Lee made a final attempt to get food for his starving troops—and he still hoped that additional Confederate forces would arrive to help him hold off the Union army. The starving, exhausted soldiers of his Army of Northern Virginia attempted a final battle against a Union cavalry unit, but when Lee discovered that the cavalry unit was backed up with two infantry units, he realized that his hope had run out.

On the morning of April 9, Lee faced his officers grimly.

"There is nothing left me but to go and see General Grant," Lee said quietly. "And I had rather die a thousand deaths."

Many of the officers' eyes filled with tears. A

young aide asked Lee what he thought history would say about him surrendering his own army.

Lee shook his head and sighed. "Hard things," he responded. Then he ordered a white flag to be raised. Surrender had finally come. The war was over.

Lee sent word of his decision to Grant, and plans were made to meet in the small village of Appomattox Court House for the signing of the articles of surrender. Grant, who had once been famous for his strict "unconditional surrender" terms, had no interest in being harsh with Lee. Like Lincoln, Grant knew that doing anything to punish the South would only hurt the rebuilding of the Union. Now, as Grant hurried toward the house where the signing would take place, he fully intended to let Lee's soldiers go home as free men. What's more, he planned to feed Lee's entire army— as much as they could eat.

When Grant arrived, Lee was waiting. Lee was dressed in a pressed, spotless commander's uniform with gold sashes and brass buttons. At his side was an engraved sword, on his hands were gray suede gloves, and his military boots had been shined until they sparkled. If he must surrender, he would surrender with dignity. General Grant, on the other hand, had not had time to change his clothes before rushing to meet General Lee. He arrived in muddy boots, wearing a uniform covered in dust and horsehair.

Somewhat embarrassed and fearing that his appearance might be taken as an insult, General Grant rushed to shake Lee's hand, hoping that he had not offended the general.

"What General Lee's feelings were, I do not know," Grant would later write. "As he was a man of much dignity, . . . his feelings . . . were entirely concealed from my observation."

Grant had no desire to do anything that might humiliate Robert E. Lee. In fact, Grant had great respect and admiration for the Confederate general. Although Grant had not agreed with the cause for which Lee had fought, he recognized Lee as a remarkable military leader. Grant insisted that Lee be treated with sincere respect. Hoping to put Lee at ease, Grant talked with him about the Mexican War, where the two men had briefly met years earlier. Finally, an awkward silence filled the room, and Lee politely reminded Grant why he had come. Then, as Grant and a group of his aides looked on quietly, Lee signed the articles of surrender that Grant had written.

After the surrender at Appomattox Court House, Robert E. Lee slowly rode his horse, Traveller, back toward his camp. When his soldiers saw Lee approaching, they began, as always, to cheer. Many mistakenly believed that he had gone to meet with Grant to tell him that he refused to surrender. However, as Lee drew closer, the cheers died down.

"As he approached," one soldier remembered, "we could see the reins hanging loose, and his head was sunk low on his breast."

When General Lee looked up, tears filled his eyes. His men knew what this meant. Quietly, a long line of soldiers began following Lee back to camp. Some men rested their hands on Traveller as they walked. Some covered their faces to hide their sobbing. Still others just stumbled along with shocked expressions.

"We had been thinking it would come to this sooner or later," an officer recalled, "but when the shock came it was terrible. Was this to be the end of all our marching and fighting for the past four years? I could not keep back the tears."

When Lee finally reached camp, the men stood in a great crowd staring at him. Lee simply walked toward his tent; then he turned, and with tears streaming down his cheeks he spoke in a trembling voice.

"Boys, I have done the best I could for you. Go home now, and if you make as good citizens as you have soldiers, you will do well, and I shall always be proud of you. Goodbye, and God bless you all."

In the Union camp, General Grant sat in his own tent, staring out grimly at the fading day. Later, he would write that the last thing he felt like doing was celebrating the defeat of a "foe who had fought so long and so valiantly, and had suffered so much for a cause." As night fell, however, some of the Union soldiers began shouting and firing their guns into the air in a show of celebration. An irate Ulysses S. Grant came charging out of his tent and ordered his men to be quiet.

"Show some respect," he said angrily, gesturing toward the silent Confederate camp. "The war is over; the Rebels are our countrymen again."

# EPILOGUE: AFTER THE WAR

$\mathscr{A}$ few days after the official surrender by the Confederacy, Union forces returned to Washington, D.C. Crowds lined Pennsylvania Avenue and cheered the 200,000 tired but smiling soldiers who paraded by.

"It seemed impossible that the boys were finally done fighting," one spectator commented. "Even after the parade was over, the crowds kept their place for a time, as if still under a spell. It was a celebration of the dawn of peace, a declaration of the re-establishment of the Union."

President Lincoln stood in a reviewing booth grinning, saluting, and waving. He looked out across the vast crowd that spilled into the streets and covered the hillsides. It seemed to Lincoln that the entire city of Washington had come out to celebrate this victorious homecoming.

But not everyone was in a happy mood. Across town, in a small bar, a young man with a handsome but brooding face sat in a dark corner drinking glass after glass of brandy. He was deep in angry and dangerous thought. He had an evil plan in mind, and he was determined to act on it very soon. His name was John Wilkes Booth.

The next morning, after a late night of fireworks and parties, Lincoln sat with his wife, Mary at breakfast. He had a strange expression on his face. When Mary asked him what was wrong, Lincoln shook his head as though trying to clear it.

"I had the strangest dream a few days ago," Lincoln finally said. It was not unusual for Lincoln to tell his wife about his dreams, but something odd in his voice troubled her.

"Strange in what way?" Mary asked, looking at her husband closely.

Lincoln proceeded to describe an eerie dream. In the dream, he had awoken in his own bed to the sound of voices and crying downstairs in the White House. But when he wandered downstairs, he could find no people, even though the sound of mourning continued. Finally, he walked into the East Room. There, a horrible sight met his eyes. Soldiers stood in a circle guarding a casket while a group of people cried pitifully.

"Who is dead in the White House?" Lincoln had asked a soldier in his dream.

"The President," the soldier replied. "He was killed by an assassin."

As soon as the soldier said this, a loud wail rose from the group of people. Lincoln had awakened at that point.

"The memory of that dream still bothers me, days later," Lincoln admitted. Mary Lincoln just stared at her husband in horror.

"What an awful dream!" she said. "It's best to forget something like that and never think of it again."

Just a few days later, however, Abraham Lincoln's nightmare would become a reality. As he and Mary sat watching a play from the presidential box at Ford's Theater, the brooding man from the bar, John Wilkes Booth, lurked just outside the door. In his pocket was a gun. Booth was a devoted Virginian and a fanatical supporter of the Confederacy. He believed that Lincoln had destroyed the South with an unfair war, and now Booth was going to destroy Lincoln. Quietly, Booth eased open the door to the presidential box and crept behind Lincoln. Just as Mary Lincoln screamed, Booth put his gun to the back of Lincoln's head and fired.

Not even a week had passed since the Civil War had ended. And now the man who was most devoted to rebuilding the South and healing the nation's wounds lay dying. All night long, the President fought for his life, but in the early morning of April 15, 1865, Abraham Lincoln died. Those gathered at his bedside bowed their heads, and Lincoln's Secretary of War, Edwin Stanton, quietly acknowledged the greatness of the man who had just passed away by saying, "Now he belongs to the ages."

The entire country was stunned by Lincoln's assassination. Some Southerners, even though they were bitter and angry about the war's outcome, wept openly when they heard the news. John Wilkes Booth had escaped to Virginia, believing that Southerners there would not only protect him, but would also honor him as a hero. He was dead wrong. Former Confederate soldiers worked alongside former Union soldiers to track Booth down. In a tobacco barn on a Virginia farm, Booth was cornered and shot.

The relationship between the North and the South was hardly friendly, however. In spite of what Lincoln had wanted, many in the North believed that the South should, in fact, be punished for the war. Southerners scoffed bitterly at this idea.

"What is left to do to us?" one man from Georgia asked angrily. "Our boys have been slaughtered, our cities burned down, our farms destroyed. What in the name of God is there left for the Yankees to do to us?"

Lincoln had planned for a period of recovery in the South that would focus on rebuilding, strengthening, and bringing the South into a new era of prosperity that did not rely on slavery. This period of recovery would be known as Reconstruction—a time of constructing a new South. However, the man who replaced Lincoln, Vice President Andrew Johnson, was a Southerner who treated Reconstruction more like restoration. In other words, Johnson was satisfied with the idea of restoring the South to the way it had been before the war.

"Damn the Negroes!" Johnson had said in frustration more than once during the Civil War. To Johnson, the war had been about overthrowing the rich plantation owners who had become traitors to the United States when they seceded from the Union. Johnson was not particularly interested in giving blacks equal rights. He felt that the Emancipation Proclamation was a waste of time that only made the war more complicated.

It may seem strange to think that Lincoln had chosen such a man to be his vice president, but Lincoln had always believed in working closely with those who held opposing ideas. Finding common ground with people you didn't agree with, Lincoln thought, was the best way to bring about real change. "When I meet a man with whom I disagree," Lincoln once said, "I want to get to know him better."

But now Johnson was President, and he was unconcerned about pushing for real change.

Furthermore, many lawmakers and Southerners blamed blacks for the terrible state that the South was in and wanted to punish them. As a way of doing so—and of making sure African Americans remained powerless—some Southern states passed what were known as "Black Codes." These were harsh laws that basically returned freed blacks to a slave state.

"Now we were called 'servants' instead of 'slaves,'" a former slave commented. "But we had no rights, still got whipped, and stayed hungry. Only difference was we were paid a penny or two. Master was still the master, though."

In Washington, the United States Congress was furious. The job of Reconstruction was taken away from President Johnson, and Congress went to work. Over the next few years, Congress did much to help blacks in the South. The Freedman's Bureau was created, and it assisted newly freed blacks with food, clothes, and medical care. More importantly, constitutional amendments were passed that outlawed slavery throughout the United States, gave African Americans the right to vote, and granted them citizenship.

Still, some people in the South could not bear to see those who had once been their property being treated as equal human beings. Others simply saw the free slaves as a reminder of the Confederacy's loss. As a result, white supremacist groups such as the Ku Klux Klan terrorized blacks by burning their homes, raping black women, and hanging men and boys from trees. Knowing that they were breaking the law, these Klan cowards hid behind masks and white robes. Their first Grand Wizard (the Klan leader) was Nathan Bedford Forrest, the same Confederate general who had ordered the slaughter of 300 black soldiers after they had surrendered at Fort Pillow.

The federal government made attempts to halt the Klan and enforce the new laws in the South, but it could only do so much. Before long, all of the advances toward equality that Congress had worked for were being entirely ignored. Southerners kept blacks from voting by quietly and systematically threatening them. They forced blacks to live in poorer conditions through the use of Jim Crow laws—laws that claimed living conditions and facilities for blacks were "separate but equal." However, facilities for blacks were never equal to those for whites.

"What does it all amount to," a frustrated Frederick Douglass asked, "if the black man, after having been made free by the letter of your law, is unable to exercise that freedom?"

It would take one hundred years for these racist laws and practices to come to an end. Not until Dr. Martin Luther King, Jr. and the civil rights movement of the 1960s would Jim Crow laws be struck down and the Ku Klux Klan shamed and subdued. And yet even after this, many African Americans would still face barrier after barrier when attempting to "exercise that freedom."

As for the South, Reconstruction officially came to an end in 1877, but the reconstruction in the South was far from complete. Much of the Deep South, where Sherman had marched, still lay in mountains of rubble. Many industries, farms, railroads, roads, and homes would not be rebuilt for many more decades. Some people believe that the South did not recover from the Civil War until the 1950s. And even today, nearly 150 years after the war's end, the economy in some parts of the South still lags behind the economy in the North.

So, what did the Civil War mean to the United States? How was it important? Certainly, it meant an end to the cruel practice of slavery. It meant the emergence of a different South. In terms of numbers, it meant nearly 700,000 young men killed over the course of four years—in more than 10,000 battles, from disease, or from other causes related to the war. It meant suffering by Americans on a larger and more horrific scale than in any other war before or since. But, perhaps most important, it also meant a new awareness and appreciation of what the United States, as a country, really is.

Before the Civil War, many Americans thought of the United States as a collection of loosely connected states, not an actual country. Then, from 1861 to 1865, hundreds of thousands of men marched throughout many of those states in an effort to keep the Union whole. They saw firsthand and in a real way how the states blend together, how the people—in spite of their differences—share so many similarities, loves, and heartaches. They saw how everyone in the country is connected.

"They walked its hills and tramped its roads," Civil War historian Shelby Foote wrote. "They saw the country and they knew they had a country. And they knew the effort that they had expended and their dead friends had expended to preserve it. It did that. The war made their country an actuality."